Free at Last

Daily Meditations by and for Inmates

The Dramatic Promise of Recovery from Substance Abuse

edited by Annette Mambuca

Hazelden
Publishing

To inmates everywhere

Hazelden
Center City, Minnesota 55012-0176

©1994 by Hazelden Foundation
All rights reserved. Originally published
1994 by Parkside Publishing Corporation
Published by Hazelden 1994
Printed in the United States of America
No portion of this publication may be
reproduced in any manner without the
written permission of the publisher

ISBN-13: 978-1-56838-070-4
ISBN-10: 1-56838-070-4

INTRODUCTION

IF THERE ARE two words that describe this book, they are "the voice." During this project, we interviewed, met with, and listened to hundreds of people, and when we finished, we realized that the voice of those who wrote this book—inmates in prison drug treatment programs —came through clear and strong. We had worried that we wouldn't be able to retain the voice. We found, instead, that it couldn't be restrained.

This book was not easy to put together. When we began, we did not know what the response would be. When we finished, people told us we had a book that could and would help many inmates. They said that we had retained "the voice."

While the details of the contributors' stories differed, their goals were always the same—to stop using alcohol and other drugs, and to break the cycle that was landing them in prison again and again. Some researchers estimate that more than 85 percent of people in prison are there for drug-related offenses, or were under the influence of alcohol or drugs when they committed their offense.

Prison drug treatment is an idea whose time has come. More than a dozen states now have such programs and many are facilitated by people who were once inmates themselves.

We believe this book can help. Whether for daily inspiration—or to provide a lead for the day's meeting—the wisdom here comes from the source. The beauty of this book lies in the voice of the many writers—a voice that is at once hopeful, sad, brave, and determined. A voice that is very real.

Acknowledgments

Parkside Publishing gratefully acknowledges the cooperation and invaluable assistance of the Gateway Foundation of Chicago, Illinois, long a pioneer in drug treatment programs in prisons. In particular, we thank Mike Darcy, Chuck Schwartz, Bob Matuzak, Bob Wiley, and Warren Buckner, all of Gateway.

Thanks to Tom McCabe for the original idea.

Thanks to Annette Mambuca for tirelessly compiling and editing this book.

Thanks to Merle Friesen, Ed.D, Director of Treatment, Alabama Department of Corrections; Mary Jones, Substance Abuse Coordinator, Louisiana State Penitentiary; and Bob Matuzak, Corrections Director, Gateway Foundation, Cook County (IL) Jail, for serving on our Editorial Advisory Board.

Thanks to Bob Kennington of Corrections Corporation of America for his invaluable expertise and assistance.

And thanks—most of all—to all the inmates who responded to our call for entries. May you receive back what you've given to others.

Prologue—Dallas T.'s Story

I WAS BORN and raised on the south side of Chicago. My mother was a single parent, so we lived with my grandparents. My home life was positive and caring. I attended St. George's elementary school and graduated from DeLaSalle High School. After I graduated, I went to work for the railroad; my father was a yard foreman and my uncle was a union steward.

At 19, I was married, had a job, and soon became the proud father of twin boys. My first real experience with drinking was at work. Most of the men I worked with were older, and there was a lot of drinking on the job. I did my best to keep up with those around me. Just a year after I went to work, I was in trouble for absenteeism due to my drinking. I wasn't fired because people covered up for me.

My mother would try to tell me that I had the responsibilities of a husband and father and shouldn't be out running the streets. But that's where I wanted to be. Although I still worked, things got progressively worse. At last I had a friend my own age at work. Unfortunately, he was using and dealing drugs. I used alcohol, heroin, and then cocaine.

My drug and alcohol use, and the need to support it, led me directly to jail. I always stole from the same place, the railroad. I would steal bed linens from the passenger train department and sell them. I continued to work, but after seven years, I lost my job.

The drinking, drugging, lying, stealing, and running around ruined my family. In the beginning, I tried hard to be a good father. As my addiction became worse, my sporadic arrests increased and my family life crumbled.

When my sons were 15 years old, my wife divorced me and moved with them to California. My next years were spent drifting in and out of jail and stealing. I would do 30 or 60 or 90 days. Jails in Vandalia, Stateville, Logan, Pontiac, and Menard were all part of my life.

I wouldn't stop using and I couldn't stay out of jail. Sentences grew longer; petty thefts became grand thefts; grand thefts became burglaries. In jail, I was a model prisoner. I helped others get their G.E.D.s.

I kept out of trouble with the gang bangers by writing their letters home. They would brag all day about what they had done on the outside but couldn't even write letters to their families. In prison, they would rather go on work crews than work on their G.E.D.s. They also wanted to keep it quiet that they couldn't read or write.

In 1982, I came in contact with the director of the Gateway Substance Abuse Treatment Center (S.A.T.C.) at the Cook County Jail in Chicago, Illinois. Jails all have rumor mills, and a friend in the jail told me the S.A.T.C. was a place where they had big bowls of marijuana that you could test out at night. I applied to enter the S.A.T.C. program right away.

My friend was wrong; the S.A.T.C. program was a place for people who admitted they were addicts. They also admitted that their drug and alcohol abuse was a large part of the reason that they were now in jail.

I was released in just 30 days and went back to the streets. I could have gone to A.A. or N.A. meetings while I was on the street, but I didn't. In A.A. they always say, "Keep coming back." I kept going back to jail.

In between jail sentences, my home was the street. I was living in abandoned buildings and cars. Sometimes I would think about my family, what they had done for me, and what they would think if they saw me. They were people who loved me, who really cared, but I chose my addictions — and now addiction controlled me.

It was horrible. I was ashamed, embarrassed, and out of control.

I had two more short-term experiences with the S.A.T.C. program, altogether about 45 days over a period of five years. Unfortunately, I was never there long enough for the program to "take."

Finally, my fourth time back, I spent 16 months in the S.A.T.C. program. I really started listening. Being confronted by my brothers in the program, I finally took a good look at myself.

I had lost everything and betrayed everyone in my life. I don't know why I was ready to listen. Maybe a Higher Power opened my ears. I was told that eventually I was going to have to get on my knees and ask for help. I said I would be too embarrassed to do that in front of the brothers in the cell. The counselor said, "Just throw your shoe under the bed, and when you get on your knees to find it, ask then."

Maybe what helped me was seeing two of the counselors in the program, Darrell H. and Warren B. They were people I'd seen coming and going in the prison system. They had been in prison ten years before, two really tough guys, and now here they were, counselors in the S.A.T.C. program, helping others. That made me think that I might be able to make it myself.

Please understand, the S.A.T.C. is still jail, but people *ask* to go there. It's cleaner; there are sheets for the beds; no violence is allowed; no one can take your food away from you. And it can be a new beginning.

In Cook County jail there are about 8,500 prisoners. In the S.A.T.C. program, there are approximately 350 people. When you complain, the staff reminds you that you are one of the fortunate ones. You asked to enter the program. Thinking about that makes it easier to do your job and go to groups and do everything else you have to do to learn how to recover. They told me that I couldn't cure my addiction, but I could do something about my thinking.

When I went to court, the director of the S.A.T.C. went with me and spoke to the judge about me. The judge asked me to tell him something that would justify his mandating me to Gateway for further treatment. I told him, "Your Honor, I am 40 years old. It's over. If I don't make it now, I'll go from the jail to the cemetery."

Today I am in the aftercare program. I'm also attending Harold Washington College. My family never gave up on me. My sons would always write and ask if I was ready to change. They are both juniors at the University of Southern California and plan to go to law school (maybe because I had so much trouble with the law).

It's been a long road. I've been clean and sober now for more than three years. I have a lot of people to thank: On behalf of my brothers and sisters at Gateway, I thank my family, the judge, and all of the staff. It takes a lot of work and good people to make good things happen.

I'll conclude by saying if I can do it, so can you.

◆

Dallas T.
Chicago, IL
April 1993

FROM THE REBELLIOUS age of 13 until my release from prison in 1981, I was in and out of various correctional institutions. Prior to my last incarceration I became a heroin addict. With heroin I found I could numb myself to the cold world I lived in, and to the people I resented and hated so much. Addiction and crime became a way of life. I hurt my family and everyone who loved me. I literally hated myself and traveled down a one-way, dead-end street with no hope for a better way of life.

Today, I thank the judge who sentenced me to prison, for he literally saved my life. Drugs almost destroyed me, but during my recovery I had to face the truth: Drugs were not my problem, only a symptom of a larger problem. I was my problem, and a Power greater than myself was in control.

After spending 27 months in a prison-based, drug treatment program, I cleaned up, got my head on straight and discovered a new freedom, a freedom within. When I was released from prison, I made a commitment to put back into society more than I had taken away. I left prison with a burning desire to be successful in my recovery and life.

◆

Bob K., Drug Program Specialist
St. Clair Correctional Facility, Alabama

JANUARY 2

TODAY MY DESIRE for recovery has become a reality. I'm proud to be a part of the solution rather than the problem, and to have 12 years clean time, a full pardon, and to be the first ex-offender hired by the Alabama Department of Corrections. I firmly believe that freedom is worth whatever price we have to pay. I now have a passion for freedom and a feeling of peace that I denied myself for many years. I was provided an opportunity to change, and I did, but I didn't do it alone.

I beat the habit and I have the victory, and I've been given a second chance at life. This time I will walk it slowly, this time I will do it right, never forgetting where I've been and how grateful I am for this life and the opportunity to help others in recovery find a positive direction in their life.

◆

Bob K., Drug Program Specialist
St. Clair Correctional Facility, Alabama

IN 1980, WHILE serving time for narcotics violations, I envisioned myself working in the field of substance abuse treatment. On June 1, 1988, my vision became reality when I was hired by the Alabama Department of Corrections (DOC) to assist in establishing the Alabama prison system's first Therapeutic Community.

I had worked in a community-based treatment program for seven years prior to working in the prison system. Needless to say, there were many adjustments. I experienced fear, apprehension, and a strong feeling of being different. I think most of the security staff who knew I was an ex-inmate felt I was still a "con" and couldn't be trusted.

It has taken me three years to abolish my fears and overcome my apprehension and the feeling of being different. Today I have established myself, gaining trust and mutual respect with the majority of the prison staff.

I am very grateful for the opportunity provided to me and wouldn't take anything in place of the challenging and rewarding work I've been involved in. I know the credibility I have established with the Alabama DOC has set a precedent for other ex-offenders hoping to utilize their experiences in recovery to help inmates who are committed to cleaning up.

◆

Bob K., Drug Program Specialist
St. Clair Correctional Facility, Alabama

January 4

STEP ONE: WE admitted we were powerless over alcohol — that our lives had become unmanageable.

The unmanageability of my life was apparent to me through the persistent decline of my livelihood and financial status. I lost my job as a result of tardiness and absenteeism. I also lost my material possessions, such as my car, furniture, and clothing. Still, I was reluctant to admit that I was powerless over my addiction.

I felt as though I could refrain from using at will. I did not fully admit my powerlessness until my exposure to recovery.

I was unaware of the deep-cutting ramifications associated with my addiction. It was difficult for me to fight an enemy I thought I knew, but really didn't. An unexpected death in the family and depression over some family matters I could not control brought to life — after 18 years — an enemy I thought I had permanently destroyed.

Now it is a battle I can win. But I have to start every day with the Steps, my powerlessness, and a willingness to let God in for that 24-hour period. When I do my life is manageable, not unmanageable

◆

Julian B., Cook County Jail, Illinois
Burglary
1 year

BEING IN RECOVERY while being incarcerated, I've learned to accept that I wasn't in control of my life. My self-image never allowed me to do that before. I portrayed a false image of a tough guy for so long that I started to believe that lie, and in doing so, I thought I was in control of my habits. In reality, I wasn't in control of anything.

Anger is what I've paid closest attention to since being in recovery. I understand that my anger has caused me much pain and grief over the years because I didn't know any proper ways to deal with it. I've learned that anger is a natural, human emotion and it's okay to get angry — it's how I react once I'm angry that matters.

I still have anger problems, but now I have better ways to deal with them other than violence. Positive self-talk and changing the way I think are the keys for me. They've saved me a lot of pain. It's not easy, but it can be done.

◆

Jeffrey G., St. Clair Correctional Facility, Alabama
Manslaughter, Assault

JANUARY 6

GROWING UP IN a rough neighborhood, I learned that to survive, I needed to be tough. I grew up viewing humble people as weak and scared.

As it turns out, the most rewarding thing I've ever changed is my definition of humility.

I now know humility to be the greatest strength a person can possess. I learned the true meaning of humility from my prison role models in recovery. The strength of humility was the one thing they all had in common.

They did have one more thing in common — they were all serious about recovery.

◆

Kelvin C., St. Clair Correctional Facility, Alabama
Robbery
Life

MY MAIN ADDICTION was sex. Even though I was putting forth an endless effort to satisfy this addiction, I knew it was wrong. I knew I was destroying myself, my wife, and my children.

I wanted to stop. I thought I could stop alone by promising myself each time that "this is the last time." I promised myself I was going to be a good father and a good husband from this day on.

Since addictions are energized by compulsion, I failed to keep my promises. This failure caused mass confusion to an already confused addict, which called for massive amounts of pills and alcohol, which only added to the problem. After hitting my rock bottom, which was being sent to prison for sex offenses with multiple life sentences, I was forced to submit to my Higher Power, God.

I had previously prayed to God for a "magic cure" to my problem. I wanted God to do it for me without any effort on my part. It didn't work that way, although my prayers were answered.

God didn't give me my instant "magic cure," but He did give me a long-term, substance abuse program, guidance, and tools for securing a new life. I'm doing it not by myself, but for myself, with the help of a lot of great people who care.

◆

James H., St. Clair Correctional Facility, Alabama
Rape, Sodomy
4 consecutive life sentences

January 8

DURING THE YEARS of my using, I never knew that I was powerless over anything. But now I understand that I am powerless over my addiction.

I'm glad that my Higher Power, whom I call God, led me to the road of recovery. One day at a time, I talk with God. I get by myself and think about the good things I can do in recovery. I meet with a friend who's also in recovery and discuss the things we will do when we get out of prison. One thing I hope to do is share what I've gone through in my life with kids who are growing up and are starting to use.

The Twelve Step program will work for anyone who wants it, but it can't work by itself. We have to be willing to work it. The program has made me happy.

I hope this helps someone somewhere who is willing to help himself or herself.

May God bless you, and may angel wings brush your pillow at night while you sleep.

◆

Douglas R., Ventress Correctional Facility, Alabama
Murder
Life

WHEN I THINK of my helplessness, it relates so much to being a prisoner. Long before I was given a cell or a dorm, I was totally confined through my addiction. I had no goals, plans, ideas, or direction.

Recovery is like a map that shows me exactly where I'm trying to go. It also allows me to see where I came from.

I've often asked myself if I can give up the driver's seat and trust my Higher Power to carry me through my recovery. I can. I've learned to let go and let God help me do all the things I never could do alone.

Now I focus on the peace that surrounds my heart by showing my thanks in every way, especially for today.

◆

Rickey W., Ventress Correctional Facility, Alabama
Robbery
25 years

JANUARY 10

AFTER LIVING 10 years in the prison system, recovery was a special challenge to me. There are certain codes we as inmates live by, such as "never expose weakness," "never allow others to know too much about you." From "jump street" I was asked questions about my past drug use. I was honest, admitting to which drugs I had used, how much, and at what age I had used them. I became honest about the earliest memories I had of my family. I didn't understand at first, but these questions and answers were part of the problem-solving process, showing where, when, and why I had become an addict.

Releasing resentments, an important part of recovery, is easy unless you try to understand why it works. I simply followed directions and felt the results. I released resentments and exposed fears, hurt, and pain. I was amazed at how quickly these things became less painful, and the resentments less important. Once I put my problems on paper and spoke about them, they moved from the inside to the outside where they could be dealt with. When I held these things inside they blocked out the sunlight of my Higher Power, as well as my sanity and reasoning. In a few days I was trusting my group and working my program.

◆

Andrew M., Ventress Correctional Facility, Alabama
Kidnapping
30 years

I SEE LIFE in a new way now. Even though I'm not "recovered" yet, I have started my journey. These Twelve Step programs really work, but only if I apply myself, use the tools, practice the principles, and am honest.

I keep it simple, follow instructions, and continue to uncover the "new" me that was there all the time. It takes hard work and courage, and none of us can do it alone. It's our choice, no one can keep us clean and sober. We make the decision to get involved and work the program.

The slogans help: Faith Without Works Is Dead; One Day at a Time; Easy Does It; Keep It Simple. Willingness, a positive attitude, and trust are the keys to sober living, one day at a time. If I can do it for one day, pretty soon I have a lot of days put together. I have recovery.

◆

Andrew M., Ventress Correctional Facility, Alabama
Kidnapping
30 years

January 12

I REMEMBER SITTING in a bar during my last time out, convinced I must be one of those poor unfortunates who are just incapable of getting this program. After all, had I not been floundering around in A.A. for more than 10 years? Had I not been through treatment three times, and read the Big Book and N.A. Basic Text more times than I could count? What was going on?

Toward the end of my journey into the dark abyss of my disease, I found myself in a detox center 800 miles from my home after making a trip that would ultimately bring me back to prison. I had called home and heard my children asking me why their daddy could not come home. On returning to my room, with tears streaming down my face, I simply said, "God, I can't take this anymore. Whoever and wherever you are, I'm going to trust you to do what I cannot."

Suddenly it dawned on me. For years I had heard, "Keep coming back, it works if you work it." The flip side to that is, "If you don't work it, it doesn't work, but keep coming back until you figure out what it is that you're not doing." For me, it was the Steps.

Today I see that the Steps not only provide a way out of the pit of my disease, but also a manner of living that is far more rewarding than anything I have ever experienced.

◆

Michael P., Ventress Correctional Facility, Alabama
Theft of property
17 years

AS WE READ the Twelve Step literature, one thing stands out above all else. This is a program that requires honesty. We must be honest with ourselves, others, and our Higher Power.

If you're like me, you've said to yourself, "Enter a drug program to get out of prison? I'll do that!" But once in the program, I realized that something was wrong with my life. After all, I was in prison, wasn't I?

I never denied I used drugs and alcohol. Being the intelligent addict that I was, I realized there was a problem and that the problem was affecting my life. But I didn't know if there was an answer to why I used drugs and alcohol. Even though I liked the feeling of being high, the hell of addiction wasn't worth the consequences I was paying.

The Twelve Steps teaches us what honesty is all about. It's not easy. It's hard to be honest about some of the things we've done. At times it will hurt to be honest; expect that pain. But like all pain, it will go away.

We can continue to play the game or we can be serious and try sobriety. Our lives are at stake.

◆

John O., Ventress Correctional Facility, Alabama
Cocaine trafficking
18 years

JANUARY 14

WE ARE PEOPLE of all ages, races, creeds, and colors. The reasons that we abused our minds and bodies may differ from one another, but the sickness is the same. We continued to rely on alcohol and drugs to hide the pain and anger that we harbored inwardly.

Those of us who have been fortunate enough to enter a treatment program should be grateful to our Higher Power for giving us maybe the one and only chance for living a sober life. There have been many alcoholics and addicts who were not allowed the luxury of getting into a treatment facility or program before they died or ended up in prison for a very long time.

Honestly speaking, the grace of God is the only reason so many of us have been spared. We are blessed to have all of our faculties still intact and functioning properly. Only through our Higher Power are we given the power to offer our experiences as some sort of spiritual motivation for those who are still controlled by their addictions. It is only by the grace of God that our mothers and fathers aren't among the many, many parents who have or will have to visit cemeteries and experience the loss of their sons and daughters. Only by the grace of God are we in recovery, with the opportunity to achieve sobriety and keep it.

Napoleon A., Ventress Correctional Facility, Alabama
Possession, cocaine and firearms
4 years

MANY TIMES IN a place like this we can find ourselves feeling lonely and depressed. Perhaps no one came to visit us this week, no one was home when we called, or we didn't receive that special letter from our loved one. We find that these are all perfect excuses to use again.

Times like these I need to search deep within and express my gratitude for what I do have. No, I didn't get a visit, no one answered the phone when I called, and I didn't receive that special letter, but today I am grateful because God has given me another beautiful day to live and enjoy. Thanks to the grace of God, I am clean and sober today.

Searching within and expressing my gratitude reminds me that the love, peace, and happiness I seek in the outside world is actually right here, right now.

If I express my gratitude, especially on those days when I am depressed and lonely, I realize just how much I have to be grateful for. In the end, I really don't have any excuses.

◆

Ignacio C., Ventress Correctional Facility, Alabama
Drug trafficking
25 years

January 16

BEFORE BEING IN recovery, my experiences with love were all fake and phony. Love was only a word to use to get what I wanted. As an addict, I found love in my drug of choice.

The program changed my outlook toward love. I came to understand the kind of love that was never-ending when others treated me with respect and concern, even after hearing my story. That's when it really started affecting me.

I had wondered how anybody could love me for my wrongdoing. But the program taught me that I am a human being, and while people may not like my behavior, they can still love me as a person. I truly see myself as an equal — nothing better, nothing less.

By the grace of God my journey has begun. For me, finding love is finding life.

◆

James B., Ventress Correctional Facility, Alabama
Murder
25 years

WHEN THE LIGHTS come on and the correctional officer shouts, "Wake up call," do we just roll over and cover our heads to block out the light and the noise? Or do we get up and begin the day with a thought of thanks for the opportunity of living, and ask God for His will to be done?

Many an opportunity has passed us by because we didn't want to wake up and take advantage of the time we had to make our lives better. It was so much easier to lay back and blame other people, places, and circumstances for our problems.

Working a program of recovery in prison, we can "wake up" and take advantage of this time to improve ourselves and our relationships with family, friends, and our Higher Power.

God is the voice that wakes me up so I may live to do His will.

◆

Thomas B., Ventress Correctional Facility, Alabama
Child abuse
10 years

ONE OF THE greatest tools I have acquired in my recovery has been "goal setting." During my years of addiction, I was a pro at setting goals, but I never finished anything I started.

Now I have begun to follow through on goals I have set. I have earned an associate's degree in science, and am working towards a bachelor's degree. I have successfully completed a drug treatment program, and I even worked for the program as an intern for almost two years. I have finished learning one technical trade and have a start on another. I have been drug/alcohol/cigarette-free for almost five years.

Yes, goal setting and goal attaining has been a great aid to my recovery. I've learned never to stop setting new goals because it's not always reaching my goals that is important, but rather the type of person I become while working toward them.

◆

Rannie C., St. Clair Correctional Facility, Alabama
Murder
45 years

I HAVE SEEN many people walk through the doors of A.A. and N.A. and never drink or drug again. I'm sorry to say that I am not one of those instant success stories. Today, I know that it was my failure to work the Steps that prevented me from being able to keep my disease in remission.

I was in and out of the program for 11 years before I decided to start working the Steps. During this time I was also in and out of jails, treatment centers, detox units, and penitentiaries. I hit many "bottoms," but only when I found myself separated from my family, hundreds of miles from home, on the run from the law with a lot of years facing me upon my return to prison, did I call out to God and work the first three Steps.

There is no way to convey in words the difference that the Steps have made in my life since that day. My Higher Power, who I choose to call God, has done things in my life that I not only *couldn't* do, but wouldn't even think to *try* to do.

Had it not been for the hell that I experienced due to my disease, I would never have found this way of life. Today, I can honestly say I'm grateful to be a recovering alcoholic and addict.

◆

Michael P., Ventress Correctional Facility, Alabama
Robbery
17 years

January 20

STEP TWO: CAME to believe that a Power greater than ourselves could restore us to sanity.

Believing that a "Power greater than ourselves could restore us to sanity" has always been a difficult concept for me to accept. It involves a matter of faith, a concept foreign to my existence.

Actually, I couldn't have been more wrong! When I sat at the bar having that drink, I had faith that if I were lonely, upset, or depressed, the drink was going to make me feel better. When I put my money through a hole in a door and received a rock or some powder in return, I had faith that it would fix me.

Perhaps you called it by a different name, but we've always had faith in a Power other than ourselves. So it's no big stretch to transfer that faith to a Power that *really* works — a Higher Power. Doing the best we can in the right way, and trusting our Higher Power on what we don't understand, makes recovery a much smoother journey.

◆

Bob P., Gateway Foundation
Lake Villa Adult Center, Illinois

STEP THREE: MADE a decision to turn our will and our lives over to the care of God as we understood Him.

I always believed that I was in control and had the power to handle "it." By "it," I meant everything from my drug and alcohol use to other people. This eventually proved to be a lie that led to disappointment, destruction, and utter despair.

The realization that I was actually out of control was in itself a blow that left me with a sense of hopelessness that brought me to my knees. My life had literally fallen apart: My marriage was over, my parents no longer trusted me, I'd lost my job, and all because of my obsession with drugs. The kicker was that I was still using — and I couldn't stop.

It was from this position of hopelessness that I was finally able to reach out for a power greater than myself for the guidance, support, and comfort that I needed. It was painfully obvious that I was incapable of managing my life. In spite of the recurrent calamities that invariably accompanied my return to drug and alcohol abuse, my continued use indicated I was insane.

The decision to turn my will and life over to the care of God in Step Three requires action and not just lip service, and the diligent working of Steps Four through Twelve.

Michael W., Ventress Correctional Facility, Alabama
Receiving stolen property, Burglary
10 years

JANUARY 22

SELF-WILL AND SELF-CENTEREDNESS — doing what "I" wanted without consideration of the rightness of the act or the effect it may have on others — is what put me where I am today. In prison.

They are a constant threat to the ongoing process of my recovery. Decisions or judgments based solely on what I want or what will satisfy me have proven to be the wrong ones. Then, not wanting to be seen unfavorably, I made more bad decisions in order to cover myself. Eventually, if not sooner, the inevitable feelings associated with my dysfunctional behavior kick in and I'm ripe for relapse.

Seeking God's will for my life through prayer (talking to God) and meditation (listening to God) affords me a sense of peace and security that I have never known. I find that the more I seek and listen to His will for me, the fewer mistakes I make. When I do make mistakes in judgment or make bad decisions, seeking God's further direction is much more profitable than the old behavior I may have once indulged in. Today I'm directed to take into consideration my shortcomings, acknowledge my mistakes, and rectify them.

◆

Michael W., Ventress Correctional Facility, Alabama
Receiving stolen property, Burglary
10 years

MOST OF MY life I've lived outside of myself. The majority of things I did or said were to impress or please other people. I had very low self-esteem and would do just about anything to be accepted by others. It was fear of rejection that led to my addiction.

After 13 years and three incarcerations, I was finally able to humble myself enough to ask for help. I entered a long-term treatment program, not having any idea what recovery was about. I sure wish recovery programs were introduced to me earlier in my life. If so, I don't think I would have led the life I did. I'm convinced that addicts cannot make it in society without some type of program to guide them.

In my four years in recovery, I have been able to reach within myself and love myself for the person I am, not the person others wanted me to be. Through listening to others in groups and A.A. meetings, I was able to start being unselfish and reach out to others.

Recovering from any type of addiction is not easy. It's a lifelong process, but along the way I'm finding that discipline and a belief in a Higher Power will take me a long way.

Let's dig down inside ourselves and reach out to other people. All we want in life is to know that someone cares.

◆

Darrell M., St. Clair Correctional Facility, Alabama
Murder
Life without parole

January 24

I CONFIRM DAILY that I'm a good guy, and that I desperately need to keep working on myself to maintain my sobriety. After being in treatment for a little over a year and a half, I still can see the importance of continuing care. Without it, I would be on the road to destruction once again.

I have learned to take the worst of any situation and turn it into a positive force that can help me along the way. Only with the help of others and the knowledge that the tough times never last — but tough people do — have I found what is needed to make it over the roadblocks of life.

◆

Ronald R., St. Clair Correctional Facility, Alabama
Receiving stolen property
30 years

MY PERSONAL EXPERIENCES in recovery have been both painful and rewarding. I've spent many arduous hours in the group process dealing with shame, anger, self-hatred, and many character defects that I denied.

I have been both a victim of sexual abuse (who became a sex addict) and a sex offender. I know the deep-rooted guilt, shame, and fear a sex addict lives with daily. It was only when I admitted my powerlessness over lust and my unmanageable life, when I got sick and tired of being in the mental and emotional state I was in, that the recovery process began healing some of the wounds of my dysfunctional life.

It was truly a tearful, painful process. But I have come to know other people just like myself who struggle with the same emotional trauma that I've worked through. I'm not alone with these problems, nor am I a worthless, bad person. I am a good person with good qualities, although I've done some bad things.

What really makes my recovery work is a spiritual awakening. As I received forgiveness from my Higher Power, I, in turn, forgave those who had abused me. All that was left was to forgive myself. Because of forgiveness, much of the anger, shame, and fear have subsided. I am very thankful for the healing of God's Spirit, and the sincere concerns of my fellow group members.

◆

James T., St. Clair Correctional Facility, Alabama
Rape, Burglary

JANUARY 26

AT A RECENT A.A. meeting we were discussing Step Nine — making amends. During this discussion one of the members told us about his repeated efforts to make amends to a family member. He had bad feelings because his efforts had not been received the way he thought they should have been.

But there can't be any selfish motives driving our amends. Most of us in prison have hurt our families repeatedly, with numerous "I'm sorrys" and "I won't do that agains," only to continue our destructive ways.

By working a program and living as God intended us to live, we have begun to earn some forgiveness. Through a concerted effort over a lifetime, we may learn to make "real" amends.

◆

Jimmy C., St. Clair Correctional Facility, Alabama
Manslaughter, Robbery
Life

IN MY WALK through recovery I have learned that without God, I cannot recover. I am incomplete without God's presence in my life.

That incompleteness, I believe, was the major cause of my addictive lifestyle. Searching to fill that emptiness caused me to waste the majority of my life in a pleasure-seeking fantasy world.

When I finally stopped looking at God as being who I had always been told He was and starting knowing God as He is to me, I found a peace and assurance that I had never known. And then true recovery began for me. For me, no spirituality means no recovery.

◆

Rannie C., St. Clair Correctional Facility, Alabama
Murder
45 years

January 28

STEP FOUR: MADE a searching and fearless moral inventory of ourselves.

I hit rock bottom after several years of imprisonment, drug and alcohol abuse, and feelings of sadness, loneliness, anger, resentment, and messed-up emotions. I was at the point of despair. I was beginning to crumble under the very situation I had created for myself.

It may sound strange, but I began working Step Four even before I knew what it was. I came into the program with mixed emotions, but I had hopes of finding some peace in my life. I felt a commitment, but it wasn't strong enough until I got a taste of recovery and a clean life.

My life began to change. At that point I stepped back and took a long, hard look at my past and the way things had turned out for me. I began to see myself as others had. It made me realize the hurt I had brought to my family and loved ones.

To me, Step Four is a must in recovery, especially if a person has veered off the straight and narrow as much as I had. Step Four broadens my perspective of my wrongs when I work it to the fullest. A great Step it is!

◆

Lee E., St. Clair Correctional Facility, Alabama
Robbery
8½ years

THE ONE WORD that stands out to me in my recovery is "courage."

I'm 38 years old, a repeat offender sentenced to life without parole, and within the last 26 months I have developed the courage to make the necessary changes in my life.

The first taste of courage came when I made a commitment to seek help. I knew that it was going to be painful dealing with my past, but I realized that my life would come to an end if I didn't change.

I was caught in the revolving door — too scared to ask for help, too scared to let on that I didn't have all the answers. What a fool I was!

Today I have the courage to deal with my problems rather than turning to drugs or alcohol. Today I have the courage to reach out for help.

Today I have courage!

◆

Larry G., St. Clair Correctional Facility, Alabama
Robbery
Life without parole

JANUARY 30

I SAW A man drunk. Boy, we all laughed at him. He was falling-down drunk. It was a sight to see. We were having just as much fun as he was.

Then the damnedest thing happened to me. I saw myself in that man. From that day on I didn't want to be drunk anymore. This was my turning point. I had been in this recovery program a good while, but seeing how he looked made me stop and think.

◆

Chandler C., St. Clair Correctional Facility, Alabama
Robbery
Life

AFTER FIVE AND a half years of incarceration, my spirituality has helped me a whole lot. Through the program, I have developed a trust and belief in God that gave me a new way of handling any situation that comes my way. It also gave me direction to help me get my goals and priorities straight.

Now that I have completed the treatment program and am living in population, I see how helpful my spirituality is in working my aftercare program. I no longer think about doing the things I used to do. My faith in God helps me think positive thoughts instead of thinking about where I'm going to get my next drug.

God, as I understand Him, has given me answers to the questions that used to send me to drinking and drugs. Spirituality was what I had been seeking.

◆

Herman M., St. Clair Correctional Facility, Alabama
Murder, Robbery
Life without parole

FEBRUARY 1

THIS MESSAGE IS to the recovering addict who may be tired of treatment centers.

I've been confined to prison for seven and a half years. It's been no bed of roses for me. I was a compulsive gambler all my life; I came to the knowledge of the truth after I entered treatment. I began my recovery nine months ago.

Enough about myself. We must first come out of denial and admit that we have an illness, whatever it may be. We then need to find a Higher Power to call on when we're feeling down and out. Our Higher Power may be God, Jesus Christ, Prophet Mohammed, or a group of people. Along with a Higher Power, we must have some confidence in ourselves.

We must never give up hope. We have to look for the good in every situation that we encounter. There's a reason for everything that happens to us, even if we don't understand what it is at the time.

Life and freedom are very special blessings from God and they can be lost on the spur of the moment. We can't look at life as a great big mystery to be solved, but rather as a unique mystery to be embraced while we are a part of it. We have to do it together.

◆

Vincent F., St. Clair Correctional Facility, Alabama
Murder
Life without parole

I'VE HAD MANY experiences in recovery. I h᠁ childhood sexual abuse, which was very painful. I had to be honest and open. At first I was afraid to open up because I thought others would look down on me. However, after I walked through all that pain, guilt, and shame, the others were right there with me the whole way. That made it easier for me to open up with the crime I had committed, but hated.

At first I thought if I told these people what I had done and with whom I had done it, they would reject me and even look down on me. I was surprised that I was not the only sex addict, and that others could share tears with me when I felt the pain of my crime. I learned it was okay to hate my crime, but not to hate myself.

I also learned that this was a family pattern that I could break. Since I had been sexually abused all of my life, I never really had a chance. I feel safe talking about all the incest, and it helps me to know that I am not alone and that I can change.

◆

John S., St. Clair Correctional Facility, Alabama
Sexual abuse
7 years

FEBRUARY 3

IT HAPPENED AGAIN today! Someone broke in front of me at chow time. That same guy bumped into me again out in the yard and didn't say "excuse me" or anything at all. The officers keep telling me to get a haircut or that I need a shave. All these things and so many more that happen cause me to feel bad. Can you identify with any of these? If you are in prison, I know you can.

When I was using and medicating my feelings, these things didn't seem to bother me so much. If it got bad enough, I would do one of two things — strike out or get high, both of which caused me plenty of problems. After 10 years in prison and more than my share of time in lock-up, I took some advice from a friend.

He told me that if I would take the time to find out what part of "me" was being affected by other people's actions, I could keep myself out of a lot of trouble. It sounded a little dumb to me because it wasn't me that was wrong, but I tried it a few times. I also discovered that I had a big image problem. I lived most of my life worrying about how other people saw me.

Now when I have a problem, I ask myself several questions before I react. Am I letting my foolish pride rule me? Am I really angry at the situation, or have my feelings been hurt? The number one truth is that I am the cause of my problems, not anyone else!

Mike H., St. Clair Correctional Facility, Alabama
Murder

FOR YEARS MY sexual addiction controlled me. I was powerless over it, and I sought pleasure in deviant sexual behavior.

But now I realize that I control my mind and body and the way I use them. I make the decision to act out; the decision does not make me. To start recovering, I first identified what I was recovering from. I know me, and I know how my mind works. I am the problem, and the solution to the problem is recovery. Do I want to hold on to my sexual behavior? I think not. And by the grace of God, I have the power of choice.

◆

Robert J., St. Clair Correctional Facility, Alabama
Sexual abuse
15 years

FEBRUARY 5

WHERE IS SHE? What is she doing? Is she still in love with me?

We have asked ourselves these questions time and time again, and we are still unsure of the answer. Having a relationship as an incarcerated person is hard. We do a lot of worrying about the other person's faithfulness to us, partly because in our active addiction, we were unfaithful.

When we make a decision to turn our will over to the care of God, we must also be ready to accept His will for us, no matter what it may be. If it is God's will that we and our companions be one, it will be.

We must remember that we have no control over other people's actions. So when we don't get a visit or a letter, we should remember that it was our own lack of control that brought us to where we are. We must do everything we can today to love ourselves, so if the opportunity to love others comes, we will be prepared.

I pray to have faith in the things I don't know. I pray for the strength to accept others.

◆

Eron L., Graham Correctional Center, Illinois
Burglary
3 years

FEAR OF NOT knowing what will happen, and the fear of failing, were my two biggest fears. But my fear was just misplaced faith.

After learning about the Twelve Step program and applying it to my life, I no longer fear making decisions, because my faith has been placed in the one thing that I know has the answers for me — my Higher Power.

Today I pray that God will continue to help me make the decision to stay clean and sober. I pray that faith will replace my fear.

◆

Steve P., Graham Correctional Center, Illinois
Auto theft
8 years

FEBRUARY 7

I'M AT MY best when I have things to do and I am doing them. My faith is evidenced to me then, because I'm doing what's expected of me as a human being and what my Higher Power expects of me.

The activity itself is not all that important. It can be anything from cleaning my cell, to legal work, but I know I am living when I can start a new project or pick up where I left off or finish something. It's an affirmation that my life is not "on hold," that I can be a creative, growing person no matter where I am. If I don't live this way, I can fall prey to boredom, moodiness, self-pity, and depression.

Activities, though, are not an escape as chemicals once were. Even though it is difficult at times, learning how to live is inspiring. It's what I've always wanted, even when I was getting high.

◆

Michael M., Graham Correctional Center, Illinois
Attempted murder, Multiple robberies

IF I COULD help someone by sharing what I went through and help them understand, this is what I'd tell them.

Life entails learning how to live. Just because we're alive doesn't mean we know how to do it. There's much involved, but the overriding factor is acceptance — accepting what occurs in our lives is everything. No matter what occurs, it has to be accepted.

Living is an individual activity; no one sees things exactly the way we do. We must define the events in our lives in a way that we can learn from them. That way, we can see the humor in a sad event, the good in some tragedy. We will know that the only thing we can control is ourselves, and that every other single thing is there for us to experience.

◆

Michael M., Graham Correctional Center, Illinois
Attempted murder, Multiple robberies

FEBRUARY 9

SOON AFTER MY arrest, when I was free on bail and awaiting sentencing for 18 months, I was fortunate to get involved with some people in A.A. who work the program in all aspects of their lives.

For that 18 months I was immersed in the program, and I had become comfortable with and accustomed to associating with people who relied on God's power and love in their lives. But when I was brought to prison, the only available bed space was in the maximum-security section.

In max, I thought that I had found a place that God had forgotten, and people that He had forgotten as well. I really knew better, however, and tried to focus on the Steps and the slogans of the program.

With God's help, and after what seemed like an eternity (10 days), I was finally transferred to the normal reception unit.

No matter where we are, or what it may feel like, God is there too. I hope I can always remember that wherever I am.

◆

Walter M., New Hampshire State Prison, New Hampshire
Theft by unauthorized taking
2 to 4 years

NOTHING LASTS FOREVER. In fact, most feelings and situations last for less than one day. Many of us go through life thinking that today's pain will last forever. In our effort to ease the pain, we turn to a substance or behavior that frequently brings more pain.

It helps me to remember that this is only one day of many, that today's problems and pain won't last forever. In fact, they will probably only hurt for today.

Being close to the time of release, I look back to my first days in prison two years ago when I thought that the end of my incarceration would never come. Now I believe that it is coming, one day at a time. Everything happens a day at a time.

◆

Walter M., New Hampshire State Prison, New Hampshire
Theft by unauthorized taking
2 to 4 years

FEBRUARY 11

I SPENT MY entire adult life focusing on what I didn't have, never looking at what I did have. If I had taken stock and been grateful for what I had, I doubt I would have embezzled from my employer.

Now my wife is gone, as is the big home, the new cars, many of my friends, and certainly my good name. Had I been truly loving and appreciative, I probably wouldn't be in prison today.

So now I am learning to be grateful. I have the love of my children, a good mind, and the lessons of my past. These are all things to be grateful for.

Some days I have to hang onto the seemingly mundane things too: that my laundry came back, that funds were transferred to my canteen account on time, that a staff member encouraged me.

If I am not grateful for everything, no matter how small, I am in danger of seeing a hole within myself that I want to fill — usually in an inappropriate way — with alcohol, drugs, gambling, sex, or material things. The best way for me to avoid these pitfalls is to recognize just how full I already am.

◆

Walter M., New Hampshire State Prison, New Hampshire
Theft by unauthorized taking
2 to 4 years

UPON ENTERING THE substance abuse program I felt out of place, because I was mandated to enter the program. On top of that, I couldn't relate to the other inmates with their drugs of choice. I remember telling myself that I wasn't an alcoholic or an addict, and that my drug of choice didn't have any affect on my life or my loved ones.

It wasn't until my fourth week into the program that the truth hit me square in the face.

This guy got up in group and shared his life story with the rest of us. It was very emotional. It sounded so much like me and the changes that had taken place in my life. It hit me so hard, that I couldn't hold back. So I volunteered to share my personal story with the group. After sharing what turned out to be a very emotional story for me, my counselor and the rest of the group pointed out to me that I had several character defects of my own. From that day on, I've applied myself to A.A. and made the Twelve Steps a major part of my life. I still have some of my defects of character, but now I know who I am and where I want to go in life.

◆

Carey A., Ventress Correctional Facility, Alabama
Burglary
30 years

FEBRUARY 13

ALL MY LIFE I've had problems trusting people outside my family. After going through the substance abuse program, I kind of felt good about myself in that area.

To do the Fifth Step, where we admit our wrongs to ourselves, God, and another person, we need that other person to be someone we can trust and feel comfortable sharing things with. I chose a guy that I considered to be a friend of mine. He was aware of the program, because we had just done eight weeks together in the same class.

Unfortunately, two days after sharing my secrets with him, the whole dorm knew. Not only did he abuse the trust I had for him, but I had a major setback in my recovery. I found it more difficult to put trust in someone than I did before.

I'm still going to do Step Five again, but maybe I'll wait until I'm on the other side of these fences. I'm confused, but not giving up.

◆

Carey A., Ventress Correctional Facility, Alabama
Burglary
30 years

I WAS 18 years old when I was sent to prison. I also was a proud father of three kids, who I loved and still love very much. But it's a different story with their mother. Since my incarceration, she married again and has tried her best to turn the kids against me. Back in the early years of my incarceration, she told me something that just rocked my world — that I didn't deserve to be the father of our kids.

That alone made me feel the lowest I've ever felt. I got to the point where I didn't care if I lived or died. I turned against myself. I hated myself. This went on for several years, until I started working the program.

I started to get to know who I really was. After I took a personal inventory and started working on my character defects, things started to happen for me. But I give all the glory to my Higher Power. Since I've let God into my life, I really feel good about myself. Me and my family still aren't as close as I would like, but I haven't given up. Why? Because of the way I feel about myself now. Now I have serenity and a Higher Power. And hope for the future.

◆

Carey A., Ventress Correctional Facility, Alabama
Burglary
30 years

FEBRUARY 15

I WAS LISTENING to this guy give his life story in the substance abuse program that I went through. After being in treatment for four weeks, I was still in denial. But some of the things he had been through I could relate to, because I had been down the same road.

That day is when my life started to change in a positive way. That's when I accepted that there was a Power greater than myself.

My personal Higher Power is my life. If there wasn't a Higher Power, I wouldn't exist. I could go on and on about what my Higher Power means to me, but I'm going to sum it up with one word: serenity.

When I'm having problems that I have trouble solving, I just turn them over and keep on striving. I'm doing it one day at a time.

◆

Carey A., Ventress Correctional Facility, Alabama
Burglary
30 years

IT SEEMS MOST of us have a great deal of difficulty admitting we were wrong, even when incarceration has us drowning in a pool of pain and struggle. Our freedom of choice may have been stripped from us, but not our ability to understand.

This is my first time in prison — a shock so intense that I feel my words alone fail to express its ramifications.

Through sobriety, however, my eyes and mind are now open. Who am I to judge another? After all, I'm not perfect, but I am sober now. I've survived my self-destructive stage during years of drinking, so prison shouldn't be insurmountable. I've learned some valuable facts about myself through the A.A. program and the gratifying Tenth Step. I can now look upon myself as another would, and humbly admit I have been wrong. I can even shout it without shame or remorse. My weaknesses of the past have now become the foundation of my strengths. Thanks, A.A.

◆

Denny N., Louisiana State Penitentiary, Louisiana
Murder
Life

FEBRUARY 17

I ALWAYS HAD a fascination for street life, enjoying things filled with excitement and chance.

Since school hardly interested me, my education was short-lived. Additionally, my first marriage failed, mainly because my heart was outside my home life. As days, weeks, months, and years passed, I found myself heavily dependent on alcohol and marijuana.

Near the close of the '80s, I became a street wizard of crack. Through observation I concluded that quick money was best earned through a scheme, even if it meant challenging both man's and God's laws.

I had much success in sales, and as time progressed, I started testing my own product. Being addicted to both alcohol and crack, my corrupt involvements led to my arrest with a history of bringing much harm and disappointments to others, particularly to my second spouse and daughter.

Upon entering prison, I immediately signed on to a drug treatment program. Steps One and Four of the Twelve Steps prepared me for sobriety and for facing up to my life's responsibilities. I'm grateful to my Higher Power that I now have two-and-a-half years of sobriety.

◆

Shirley N., Louisiana State Penitentiary, Louisiana
Distribution of drugs
7 years

ONE OF THE biggest obstacles to change and recovery is the ego. Our ego won't let us admit that we have no control over people, places, and things. And until we do, we'll always fight a losing battle. Thinking we have control over our addiction always led us to do more "research."

Yet when the guard yells "Lock-up," we're confronted with our powerlessness. As we look through the bars at a beautiful day, longing to be with our loved ones, we acquire an intimate knowledge of our powerlessness. We can no longer deceive ourselves.

Refusing to admit our lack of control over our addiction has doomed us to a lifetime of misery. Addiction is the only war in which we must surrender to win. The First Step in recovery is to admit, without reservation, our powerlessness.

As we grow in our recovery, we learn that although we may not be able to control people, places, and things, we can control our responses to them.

◆

Bob P., Gateway Foundation
Lake Villa Adult Center, Illinois

FEBRUARY 19

TO MANY OF us in active addiction, integrity was a foreign word. There was no set standard that we followed; everything could and would be compromised according to the needs of the moment. True, in prison there was an expected code of behavior, yet often it was contrary to our inner selves. So again we compromised our integrity.

To change, we must establish and adhere to our own system of values. Something is either right or it's wrong; there can't be any "in-between." We must learn to trust ourselves and march to the beat of our own drummer.

Having integrity means adopting principles of living where right and wrong are sharply defined. It's a simple concept to understand, but it's not necessarily easy to establish. The payback or rewards may be slow in coming, but we'll realize an inner harmony knowing we're finally doing the right things for the right reasons.

◆

Bob P., Gateway Foundation
Lake Villa Adult Center, Illinois

As WE BECOME involved in our recovery, listening to the different messages and trying to apply them in our lives, a tendency to hurry up the process develops. The results we're seeking are not readily discernible. We revert back to our addictive thinking wherein "we want what we want when we want it."

But even that is an illusion, for we've been waiting all our lives. We waited on the "dope man." We waited all day in courtroom bullpens for a two minute hearing with the judge. We waited on the guards to open our cells. We waited on chow lines, sick-call lines, and especially on the parole board. Waiting has been an integral part of our lives.

In recovery we learn to undo the many years of our negative lifestyles. The process cannot be hurried. It's one step at a time, one day at a time. If we work our program, we'll see that things will open up for us when we're ready.

Recovery is a lifelong process. We must be patient to realize its rewards.

◆

Bob P., Gateway Foundation
Lake Villa Adult Center, Illinois

FEBRUARY 21

THERE'S NEVER BEEN any room in our lives for humility. Our lifestyles dictated that this was a sign of weakness. We employed arrogance in its place. Our addiction was a closed circle, and our arrogance further encapsulated us.

In our arrogance we thought we had all the answers. We knew all we needed to know to do the things we did. Thus we couldn't learn to change, even if we wanted to.

Arrogance is like having a full cup of water; nothing else can be added. Humility, on the hand, is having the cup half-filled. Being humble means one can always learn something new and is capable of change.

Humility is a part of recovery. It lets us admit that we don't have all the answers — that we may not even know all the questions. It allows us to seek and receive help with our addictions where we can. It prepares us for change.

◆

Bob P., Gateway Foundation
Lake Villa Adult Center, Illinois

LIVING A LIFE of recovery is much more than simply not drinking or drugging. We must change our way of doing things. We must change the way we treat other people. Learning to accept that things are the way they are right now because that's the way they are supposed to be is tough.

It can get better — or worse — depending on how we choose to conduct our lives from this very moment on.

Just not drinking and drugging will not change our lives. That is the first step, of course, but becoming the type of person who has self-respect, is honest, and cares for others is the real key to recovery.

Let's not just dry out, but truly clean our lives up by working a true recovery program each and every day.

◆

Rannie C., St. Clair Correctional Facility, Alabama
Murder
45 years

FEBRUARY 23

I ENTERED THE penitentiary when I was 19 years old. I was sentenced to 19 years for possession with the intent to distribute cocaine. Yes, my hustling days were over. What I didn't realize was that my struggle for my freedom from addiction was just beginning. I didn't know what to expect in prison. The only thing that was on my mind was, "I want to get out."

I was a cocaine user. At first it wasn't hard for me to support my habit, but as life caught up with me, it became more expensive. When I had drugs, money, and a car, I had plenty of so-called friends.

But in jail, Monday through Friday I would sit on my bed, and listen to the officer calling the names of the people who had mail. The first letter I received was from my mother; nothing from my "friends." I realized how much my mother loved me. I regret every little mistake I made to make my mother feel bad.

I had always denied using drugs. I could have fooled the whole world except for one person, and that's God. Fortunately, He gave me a second chance. Now in rehabilitation, I plan to further my education and help my family in every way I can.

The best thing I can tell all you teenagers out there is to say no to drugs and stay in school. Peace, brothers and sisters. You are the friends I can rely on today.

◆

Benito R., St. Brides Correctional Center, Virginia
Possession with intent to distribute cocaine
19 years

WE HAVE A philosophy here in the treatment program that we recite twice a day. The part that has really affected my life is, "We have awakened to realize that where we are in our lives is not where we want to be." Before treatment and recovery, even though I was headed for destruction, I thought I was in control of my life. When I became aware of my condition I realized that my life was unmanageable and out of control.

On January 14, 1983, I received a life sentence without parole as an habitual offender. This was an awakening for me, because as I inventoried my life, I couldn't see anything but a man who failed at the most menial tasks. My self-esteem had been corrupted by failure. The talents I had were wasted through misuse. I refused to accept the consequences of my own petty thoughts and lazy deeds, so I searched for a scapegoat to blame.

Since being in recovery I have learned that I can be anything I want to be, but not without sacrifice, dedication, commitment, and a strong determination. I'll find myself again. Failure and despair will never be my choice. I will choose success and happiness. Recovery is a way of life for me now, and it has given me a new life that's much more fulfilling and rewarding than anything I've ever had before.

◆

Kenneth G., St. Clair Correctional Facility, Alabama
Robbery
Life without parole

STEP TWO: CAME to believe that a Power greater than ourselves could restore us to sanity.

What is not apparent to the addict is that a Power greater than himself and his drug of choice can restore him to sanity. It takes a personal experience of spiritual enlightenment to humble the addict.

I encountered a major spiritual experience after praying and fasting in prison. I was severely depressed after receiving 10-30 years for armed robbery, and I began to call on my God. And He answered me. I personally believe that I can prevent trauma and certain hardships in my life if I turn my will and my life over to the care of God. With this belief comes faith and with faith comes humility.

My most intellectual thinking is what led me into addiction. Once I got my own thinking out of the way and relied on God, I came to believe that a Power greater than myself would restore me to sanity.

◆

Julian B., Cook County Jail, Illinois
Burglary

IT'S BEEN A long, tough road that led me to where I am today. The first time I came through these gates was in 1968; now it's 1992.

When I went to my initial classification, I was told they had a drug program. I didn't care about the program, but it meant being housed closer to home so I signed up. I didn't know then it was the beginning of a new life for me. I really never thought I had a problem with drugs because I could go for periods of time without using. Thanks to God, my Higher Power, I know exactly what I am. I'm in prison, yet I feel freer than ever before. It feels like all the weight has been lifted off my shoulders.

For so many years I thought I had all the answers. I'm now sitting back and listening to what other recovering people are saying.

It's taken me 46 years to get where I am and I know I've got a long way to go, but I'm on my way "one day at a time." I will be released very soon and am going to a recovery house. I know how very fragile I am right now. I'm more than willing to give six months or however long it takes to build a foundation for a lifetime of recovery. I know it's not going to be easy, but I'll be around people just like myself who will love and understand me.

◆

Diane L., California Institution for Women, California
Forgery
16 months

I STARTED USING cocaine many years ago as a pastime on weekends. As time went by, I found myself using more drugs — not only on weekends — but on any day I wanted to feel good. I never thought I was addicted. I thought because I came from a good family, I was different. As my addiction progressed, I abandoned my friends and started hanging out with people who used. I didn't see how much I had changed. I always thought I was in control. I was the queen of rationalization; I always had a reason for my use.

I led myself to believe I wasn't an addict because of things I didn't do to get drugs; I never looked at the things I did do or the situations I put myself in.

The hardest Step for me in the Twelve Step program was Step One. For me to admit I was powerless and my life was out of control was really hard, because it boiled down to admitting I was an addict. After I accepted Step One, the others were easy. I started to feel better about myself, because I knew the cause of some of my problems. The biggest obstacle for me in my recovery is looking at my shortcomings and all my character defects. The thought that keeps me going in my recovery is knowing I'm not perfect and don't have to be.

These are the things that have led to my spiritual awakening.

◆

Debbie B., California Institution for Women, California
2 years

MY PARTICIPATION IN N.A. while in this period of incarceration has given me a new awareness of the word "enough." N.A. has taught me to say "Enough" to myself. I can now say good-bye to negative people, unhealthy places, and debilitating things.

In order to deal with a weakness effectively, one needs to be aware of that weakness. Once it's acknowledged, we can admit powerlessness over it. In working Steps One, Two and Three, I've learned to say "Enough" to my life being managed by drugs. I can now walk away from destructive behaviors and the many years of foolishness.

None of this could have been done alone. Thanks to my Higher Power and Narcotics Anonymous, I didn't have to go it alone. The best way to learn how to say "Enough" to myself is to attend meetings regularly, work the Twelve Steps of Narcotics Anonymous, and read and study N.A. literature. These are the things that lead to a good and productive life in recovery.

◆

Eddie S., Logan Correctional Center, Illinois
Possession of a controlled substance
8 years

FEBRUARY 29

STEP NINE: MADE direct amends to such people wherever possible, except when to do so would injure them or others.

Step Nine really worried me at first, but not because of what the Step actually instructed — making amends. God and I know that I hurt a lot of people through my addictions. Step Nine scared me at first because it didn't guarantee that once I made amends to those that I'd harmed, they, in return, would automatically forgive me.

In reality, all the people I've hurt won't forgive me. But the thing I have to recognize is that for once, getting and giving forgiveness matters to me.

◆

Jerry W., St. Clair Correctional Facility, Alabama
Robbery, Escape
Life

WITHIN THE STRUCTURE of the prison drug program, we are taught a variety of ways to identify and confront negative behavior patterns in each other without violating the rules of the structure. Some of these coping skills are termed "house tools." If one client offends another in some way, this is called "creating feelings." And the person who was offended can talk to the individual on a one-on-one basis. Or he can "book" the offender by writing on a booking slip the rule that was violated, then confront the individual in "cluster," where the people involved iron out their differences before the inmate family.

Well, God must have, at one time or the other, been a member of this program. He tried many times to talk to me "one-on-one" to try to steer me away from my negative behavior. But I didn't listen. I held the course of my addiction steady. So God was offended and "booked" me for not keeping His rules.

God is prepared and willing to bless me beyond measure. After God read me my "booking," I ignored Him still, so he felt the need to bring me to "cluster group." Now that I'm incarcerated, He's trying to get one-on-one with me again. This time I'm listening.

◆

Julian B., Cook County Jail, Illinois
Burglary
1 year

MARCH 2

I HAD BEEN in Twelve Step programs (A.A., N.A., C.A.) for about five years. I tried to make 30 meetings in 30 days, but always fell short. I just never really connected. I knew all the Steps, phrases, and sayings in my head, but I never got them in my heart.

Sometime in 1988 at a Cocaine Anonymous meeting, I finally learned the real meaning of the saying, "One day at a time."

I started telling myself I'd get high tomorrow, but not today. When tomorrow came I'd tell myself again, "I won't get high today, I'll get high tomorrow." As the months went by, it got easier and easier. Over the last four years it has worked better and better.

Maybe my version of "one day at a time" isn't the original meaning, but it still works for me. I don't say it will work for everybody, but if nothing else is working, give it a try. Maybe in the next four to five years I can learn my own "true meaning" of something else in the program.

◆

Robinson H., Nottaway Correctional Center, Virginia
Armed robbery, Burglary, Forgery
30 years

IN OUR TWELVE Step meetings, an interesting question arose dealing with the Fourth Step: "Made a searching and fearless moral inventory of ourselves." What is moral? What some feel is immoral, others may disagree.

When I have difficulty distinguishing right from wrong, I ask myself these questions. Would my actions offend someone? Will my words (even though true) upset the listener? Am I hurting myself by doing this? Are the questionable acts of my peers detrimental to my well-being or self-improvement? If the answer is yes to any of these, perhaps a different approach would be better.

The key to success in any endeavor is to eliminate the negative and accentuate the positive. Then, making that fearless moral inventory isn't such an arduous task.

◆

Denny N., Louisiana State Penitentiary, Louisiana
Murder
Life

MARCH 4

FOR THE REROUNDER who wants to get sober, a personal inventory is important. We must look back on our behavior, focusing on the precise moment when the thought about using again surfaced. We must keep ourselves under constant scrutiny during the course of treatment.

Direct changes in certain behavior patterns must be paramount to all else. Constant reflection as to what we did and what we will do differently this time to prevent relapse is very important.

The precise moment of temptation will come again. What helps most is a good strong spiritual base. God is a very present help in times of potential relapse. When we have a good spiritual base and a mind made up to stop suffering, we are on the road to recovery again.

◆

Julian B., Cook County Jail, Illinois
Burglary
1 year

I FIRST CAME to prison in 1988 with a charge of possession for sale and did a 16-month term. Since then I've been back on four violations, each time for drug-related and prostitution charges.

When I was in the county jail, I found out about the substance abuse program and thought I might as well give it a try. The first month in the program I sat back and wouldn't participate. One day a counselor said something that I could relate to, and I started opening up. I've been sharing ever since. I now know my warning signs and triggers for relapse.

Men are one of my triggers because I was only attracted to the ones who lived the same kind of lifestyle that I lived. Now that I know what makes me relapse, I am doing something about it.

I am going into a sober-living home after I finish my program here because if I want to stay clean, I need to put as much effort into being clean and sober as I did into doing drugs and prostitution. I don't care if it takes a lifetime, I'm going to make it. I have my Higher Power and my support group to help me.

◆

Cherry S., California Institution for Women, California
Parole violation
1 year

MARCH 6

SPIRITUALITY — KNOWING THAT a Power greater than myself could restore my mind to sanity — has played a major role in my cleaning-up process. Praying and meditating have enabled me to receive strength and helped me to focus on priorities that needed my complete attention.

I also asked God to give me strength to take one day at a time. Through daily prayer and meditation, I realized that in order to have a successful program, I would need a balance. This balance has enabled me to work a recovery program knowing that God is the center or core, and that He is responsible for the help I'm now receiving. It has helped me understand the meaning of a Power greater than myself.

◆

Ronald H., St. Clair Correctional Facility, Alabama
Robbery
7 years

WHEN I STARTED serving my 19-year sentence at a county jail, keeping my mind off drugs was not hard at all. A couple of months later, I was transferred. There I would listen to my fellow inmates talk about cocaine and all other kind of drugs, but drugs never came into my possession.

A few months later, I was transferred. The years I spent in county jails and receiving units, I had been free from drugs. Once at this other prison, however, I started seeing all kinds of drugs floating around like it was nothing. It gave me flashbacks, but I had a lot of faith in myself, and more importantly, in God.

Many guys would ask me to get high with them, but thank God I learned that powerful phrase, "No, thank you." My current prison for the drug treatment program helped me understand facts about life and what cocaine does to a person.

These past years of incarceration have been the best in my whole life. To all teenagers who are reading this, please don't think that I made it up. This is reality. You don't have to enter a penitentiary to learn everything I learned. You can be whoever you want to be. All you have to do is believe in yourself and have faith in a Higher Power. I don't care whether you're black, white, Jewish, or Catholic. We all come from the same place.

◆

Benito R., St. Brides Correctional Center, Virginia
Selling cocaine
19 years

MARCH 8

A NEGATIVE HABIT of many addicts is a desire to get everything done quickly. The powerful force of addiction drives us addicts to satisfy our craving as soon as possible and by any means possible.

It is true that certain circumstances may call for hurried action, such as helping someone escape from a fire or rushing to turn off the stove when food is burning. But in general, life does not require hasty actions.

We who are incarcerated must be especially careful. In a restricted and controlled environment, it's easy to get seriously depressed. A key element to acquiring patience within the system is to follow protocol. Trying to take the shortcut and get to the top quickly is the basic reason most dope dealers sell drugs.

In recovery, the slogan "one day at a time" has a special meaning to me. It helps me slow down, take it easy, and stay sober and clean. I don't have to do everything *right now*.

◆

Julian B., Cook County Jail, Illinois
Burglary
1 year

DURING MY ADDICTION I pointed the finger of blame at many people and things: my parents, my friends, my past, my environment. Every time I hit my wife, I blamed it on my dad because he hit my mom. Every time I got drunk, I blamed it on my mom because she was an alcoholic. Every time I got into trouble, I blamed it on my friends. Every time I went to prison, I blamed it on my environment.

One day I sat down and wondered who my son was going to blame if he went to prison or became an alcoholic or beat his wife. Who were his kids going to blame their troubles on? Sure, I could blame just about every wrong thing I've ever done on a lot of people from my past, my son could blame his troubles on me, and so forth. But all I'd have is a whole bunch of people pointing fingers.

The fact of the matter is, I'm an alcoholic and I'm the one in prison. No matter who I blame, I'm the one who has to live with that. Not my wife-beating father or my alcoholic mom or my friends who are a bad influence, but me. So I came to a conclusion: I can keep pointing my finger at other people and remain an alcoholic and keep coming to prison, or I can walk up to the mirror and point the finger at myself. As soon as I did, I took the first step toward recovery.

◆

Johnny E., Graham Correctional Center, Illinois
3 years

MARCH 10

AN ADDICT IS sick and needs help. He cannot go to his friends because somewhere down the line he has betrayed them. He cannot go to his relatives, because somewhere down the line he has let them down. He cannot go to the community, because the community has labeled him the scum of the earth.

God in His omnipotent power knows all about our struggles. In fact, He may have sent some our way in order to cause us to humble ourselves. God created us, and He knows us.

A person who lacks a spiritual foundation may not readily recognize God's voice talking to him. I could have been headed for danger and God tried to get my attention by creating certain circumstances in my life to slow me down. I may have had many warnings, but I failed to heed them. God knows what size shoe I wear physically and spiritually. He knows what it will take to humble me. For some of us, it will take a major trauma or hardship to take heed, like a severe illness or accident. For others, it will take a prison term. Nevertheless, we can rejoice because God's love transcends prison bars and doors.

◆

Julian B., Cook County Jail, Illinois
Burglary
1 year

EACH DAY THAT passes brings me closer to my power-lessness. When I feel frightened and caged and anxiety sets in, the only peace I can find is in my First Step book. As I read, inner peace comes — an inner peace I never felt on the streets.

Truth is often unpleasant. The truth that my drug problem got me here is very painful; realizing I'm powerless over my situation may hurt — but it can set me free.

Accepting that I'm powerless over my life and the people in it causes me indescribable pain, especially when I think of my family and how much I miss and love them. But I thank God every day for my recovery program. Because without it, I would surely die.

◆

Rosita S., Dwight Correctional Facility, Illinois
Attempted murder, Shoplifting
20 years

MARCH 12

IN RECOVERY, I have finally learned how to communicate with other people. I have learned that the people in my program are my friends and family, and that many are just like me. I have learned to be honest and to love people, no matter what they have done.

The people here love me. At first I could not understand why anyone would want to help me, much less love me. But they really do, and I thank God for every one of them.

My number one goal is to complete the program and get everything out of it I can. Then, if and when I go to the free world, I want to take what I have learned and freely give it to anyone who wants and needs help.

The program has given me a reason to stop what I was doing in the past. It has given me love, and I want to share my love and help with others.

◆

Albert S., St. Clair Correctional Facility, Alabama
Robbery
30 years

ON OCTOBER 22, 1991, after being captured after an armed robbery, I surrendered my life to my Higher Power.

For years I have been running from God through drugs and alcohol. I'd been fortunate enough to play football on a college and professional level, yet there was always a void inside me. When I asked my Higher Power into my heart that day, all my burdens were lifted and I gained hope in life.

I'm now serving a 45-year sentence in prison for armed robbery, but today I am free! I still have many character defects and hidden anger, but overall I know that through working my program in recovery and seeking my Higher Power daily, I can live a sober life. By praying, reading, and sharing, I can help others. By helping others, I can also help myself. And for that I am grateful.

◆

Joe K., St. Clair Correctional Facility, Alabama
Armed robbery
45 years

NUARY 14, 1992, I have been clean and sober, and it is due to my recovery program and God. I can't have one without the other.

My Higher Power, whom I choose to call God, has given me contentment. Even if I was never to get out of this prison, today I truly know I am free within. When all else fails and when all friends and family have given up on me, I know I have a true Friend who walks with me daily. Without God, I would still be in that merry-go-round lifestyle.

◆

Joe K., St. Clair Correctional Facility, Alabama
Armed robbery
45 years

SUBSTANCE ABUSE PROGRAMS are new to me, even though I've been in this prison three times before. The times that I've been here before I was very active in the drug scene, and now I carry a few physical scars as well as mental scars. Since I've joined A.A., I have overcome the grip that bound me to drugs and alcohol. I am even helping others get started in Alcoholics Anonymous and substance abuse treatment programs. It makes me feel good to know that I can and do help others overcome their hurdles.

At times I get a bit discouraged, you know, down on myself. That's when I look back on my past life and look at others who are in the same situation now, and somehow that inspires me. It drives me to help those who are willing to make changes. For those who are not yet ready, I hope to plant the seed.

I feel that the Alcoholics Anonymous and substance abuse programs are very beneficial to those who are incarcerated and willing to change. Furthermore, I will assist in almost any way to better A.A. or even create new self-help programs to help those who wish to help themselves.

◆

Albert C., Louisiana State Penitentiary, Louisiana
Sexual battery
40 years

IT'S ALWAYS CONFUSING when we are in a relationship with someone and we don't know where we stand, regardless of what type of relationship it might be. For years I was afraid to get into relationships with other people because I didn't know how to set boundaries for a healthy relationship. As a result, I was always getting hurt through rejection or through not being able to live up to certain expectations or vice versa.

It eventually reached a point where I was unable to sustain a relationship with anyone. At this point, I reached rock bottom. I began to search for a definition for life and relationships. Through my involvement in the recovery process, I began to see how unhealthy all my relationships had been, and I noticed a very simple concept that was always missing. The missing ingredient was honesty. Once I began to be honest, I enjoyed developing relationships with friends, family, and others.

◆

Timothy C., St. Clair Correctional Facility, Alabama
Murder

SOMETIMES WE CAN learn from other's mistakes as well as our own. Even so, we must not expect ourselves or others to always be there, because we have failed ourselves before and others have failed us. But God never will.

To walk spiritually with God, all we have to do is believe and have faith, then be patient and wait for God to give us what we need. We must learn to let God have complete control, and trust in Him to help us.

Always remember, whoever walks along God's true path of recovery will never be alone. All who trust in God will be blessed with the fruits of the Spirit — love, peace, joy, gentleness, goodness, faith, and meekness.

God is my spiritual help in times of trouble. God is my refuge and my strength. I put all my trust in God.

◆

Tommy C., Elmore Correctional Center, Alabama
Sale of a controlled substance
5 years

MARCH 18

HYPOCRISY, VANITY, LYING, and fear are the things that make our souls prisoners.

When we live united with these feelings, depression comes, along with suffering and insecurity within ourselves. Then we resort to alcohol and drugs as a means of escape. And in this manner, we transgress to a worse state: infidelity, hatred, scornfulness, pain, and crime. Later come the final steps — the hospital, the prison, and the cemetery.

We must ask a Higher Power, without lying or hypocrisy, to give us the strength and courage to cleanse our souls. Because when we free our souls, we have serenity and happiness.

◆

Maximo G., Cook County Jail, Illinois
Possession of a controlled substance and a firearm

LIVING A LIFE of recovery is impossible without a Higher Power. We must realize that we cannot recover by ourselves. We must humble ourselves enough to ask for help.

My Higher Power is that little voice in my head that says, "Don't do that" or "Be strong for just one more day." Through meditation I have become at one with my Higher Power. Whenever I feel as though I am going to relapse, if I need encouragement, or even if I need a good scolding, I can hear His voice.

Do I heed the things my Higher Power says? God, help me to hear and understand the things You say to me, and to act upon Your wisdom.

◆

Johnni W., Lee Arrendale Correctional Institute, Georgia
Aggravated assault

March 20

RECOVERY IS NEVER easy, but I feel I made the right decision to get help before I'm released on parole. My belief is no one can help me unless I want to help and change myself.

The hardest thing I have to deal with at this point in my recovery is anger. I feel I have come a long way with helping myself. I have to finally realize that I can't get mad unless I make myself mad. Once I learn to control my anger and show my feelings in a healthy way, I'll get along in society better.

Personally I feel that if the Twelve Steps could help me, they can help anybody. My self-esteem is a lot higher now than when I was using drugs. I hit rock bottom five or six times, and I finally think I'm going to make it with what I learned from treatment. As far as my Higher Power is concerned, He plays an important part in helping me make important decisions. He often works through other people around me. He can work through anybody.

The most important things in my life at this point and time are my sobriety, not forgetting where I come from, and not to be incarcerated again. But all I have learned is no good unless I give it to others. That way I will keep growing.

◆

Jimmy H., Lee Arrendale Correctional Institute, Georgia
Aggravated assault

IN THE PROGRAM we are taught discipline. We are structured so that we may govern ourselves. But because we are all addicts, we got out of hand. Residents went through the day trying to "bust" as many people as possible. Somewhere along the line we all missed hearing the counselor saying that this was a treatment program, not boot camp.

Now, each day I have to double-check my motives if I am going to help someone. I have to think about the reason I am going to bring something to a fellow resident's awareness. Am I doing this to help, or is it for personal satisfaction?

◆

Shawn K., Lee Arrendale Correctional Institute, Georgia
Auto theft

MARCH 22

IN THE RECOVERY program that I'm participating in, I really had to find myself. I had the ability to love myself and care for others, but there's still a lot I have to work on.

As for defiance, my attitude is well-balanced. I don't have any hatred toward anyone, but I know when I get irritated toward something, I normally isolate myself. Maybe that's wrong, but it seems I can handle it better that way. When it comes to authority, at times I have to admit I'm powerless over things I can't change. But that's just what we have to go through in life.

Because of my addiction I lost my father, so that's something I look at as a reminder. As I move further on in life, my goal is to share with other kids and adults what I've experienced. That way I'll have something to be proud of.

◆

Charles J., Lee Arrendale Correctional Institute, Georgia
Murder
Life

I AM PRESENTLY serving time for a robbery borne out of my need to support my drug habit. I remember a time when all I would do was run drugs. There was no exception to who I sold to or bought from, because in the drug race, there are no moral principles.

I don't blame anyone for what has happened to me. Today, I finally understand why my family and friends turned against me. It wasn't because they didn't love me; they tried to teach me about life and real love, but they did it their way.

I've seen a lot of families destroyed as a result of drugs. The suicidal missions that drugs lead to can include stealing from loved ones, shoplifting, or pawning everything you own. Destruction is inevitable.

I had never been to prison for drugs before, but during this incarceration I found myself moving toward recovery as a result of my prison experience. And I have friends who give me books and continue to make efforts to steer me in the right direction.

My life has been a series of trials and errors — serious errors — because drugs kept me from correcting my mistakes. The fool in me kept making the same mistake over and over and over again. That is why drugs are so destructive.

◆

Roland R., Louisiana State Penitentiary, Louisiana
Robbery
20 years

MARCH 24

THERE ARE MANY people I would like to thank for reaching out to me and assisting in my recovery. Through their help, especially members of my family, I've learned much about myself.

Of course, my experience won't necessarily steer another from the use of drugs; it just doesn't work that way. There has to be that inner drive or some personal affliction that causes people to change. It's not just a want or a desire to change, it becomes a demand, a will to rise above the state of being we're in. Our drug problem has to somehow affect us in a strong way, perhaps destroying something or someone who means more to us than we mean to ourselves. But how many are strong enough to attempt recovery before a loss occurs? Intelligence has absolutely nothing to do with it.

I think that the only real teaching is by experience. I know that drugs are not for me because of their destructiveness. I understand now that I was vulnerable to every temptation that confronted me. The last 10 years have lent me some rich experiences which gave purpose to my life. I am so appreciative to all of the people who have lent a hand to lift me from the gutter so that I may have a chance to live again.

◆

Roland R., Louisiana State Penitentiary, Louisiana
Robbery
20 years

I DON'T REALLY know what to say, but I'm going to try and talk from my heart. I know that it's hard to stop using drugs, but you can do it, and it will make you a better person. You will feel good about yourself and others around you.

Don't be like me. See, I used drugs until I lost all of my thinking power. I was having so many problems I just didn't know what to do. So I turned to crack to keep me going, and before long, I was hooked. It got so bad that I stopped thinking, and started listening to that rock talk to me.

It talked me all the way to death row. Now I may lose my life, and for what? Did drugs solve my problem? Do they solve yours? I don't think so, they only made them worse. There is help for us, but we must want to get better. The Twelve Steps are a way to really find ourselves and the power of God. But we have to want to do it.

◆

Feltus T., Louisiana State Penitentiary, Louisiana
Murder
Death penalty

MARCH 26

IT'S NOT ENOUGH to recover just because it may help us get out of prison sooner. Why get out sooner if we're going back to the same old life that got us to prison in the first place? We have the time now to better ourselves, so let's do it.

If we work the Twelve Steps and want to recover, a Higher Power will be there to help us along, and we will leave prison as much better people. We'll be able to help someone else who's out there on drugs, making a mess of their life. So, my friends, let's help ourselves so we can help someone else. Isn't that what it's all about, sharing something that has worked for us so it can help someone else?

We can change, but we have to want to change. When we feel that we can't go on, we need to remember that God is by our side. All we have to do is call and He will answer. Try it today, tomorrow may be too late. Don't wait any longer, do it now! The Twelve Steps can change our lives.

I know it's hard, but you can do it. I have faith in you, and that is what you must have in yourself. Don't let what happened to me happen to you!

◆

Feltus T., Louisiana State Penitentiary, Louisiana
Murder
Death penalty

THERE ARE PROBABLY as many excuses as to why people abuse drugs as there are drugs to abuse. But regardless of the excuses, the end result is usually the same — the destruction of one's self-esteem. Drug addiction is a process that removes an individual from reality and exposes them to another dimension of life. The problem is, it's a fabricated life filled with delusions, deception, and disappointment that denies a person any self-control.

Abusing drugs is easy, overcoming drugs' control over our lives is something else. Not everyone has the opportunity or accessibility to the various treatment options that are available to addicts, nor is there any guarantee of success for those who do. And regardless of whether we have family and friends for support, treatment programs to attend, or spiritual backing from our church, none of those means of support can be of any substantial help unless and until we can admit to ourselves and others that we need help and are determined, at whatever the sacrifice, to overcome our addiction.

In essence, we are the primary source by which we control our own lives.

◆

Jon S., Louisiana State Penitentiary, Louisiana
Aggravated robbery, Aggravated burglary, Car theft
231 years

MARCH 28

BREAKING FREE FROM an addiction can be a struggle and a real test of nerves. Naturally, just thinking about it won't get the job done. We must be willing to respond in every way possible to an unyielding ego, because drug addicts find it easier to submit to the addiction than to resist.

After all, no one likes making radical transitions. But even if it means sacrificing our present lifestyle, environment, or certain friends, our lives are worth it. Recovery is merely a matter of convincing ourselves that we want our lives back, and not taking "no" for an answer. Keep in mind that we must never accept defeat from an enemy we have the ability to control.

If we keep focused on our goals and maintain a positive attitude each and every day, we can participate in the healing process that will inevitably lead to recovery.

There is still hope for us to regain control of our lives. But it has to be a life that we want more than anything else. A life that is totally free from all outside interference. We must use our God-given abilities and strengths to take back what's rightfully ours, and use each day to reflect on life's goodness and how we are the ones who control what life will be like for us.

◆

Jon S., Louisiana State Penitentiary, Louisiana
Aggravated robbery, Aggravated burglary, Car theft
231 years

SEVEN YEARS AGO I was on my third escape. I had used and abused all the people who loved and cared about me in my pursuit for drugs and freedom. I didn't care about anyone but myself, didn't stop to think about anyone's feelings but my own, and I couldn't see nor did I care about the pain I caused others by my actions.

As I sat in a six-foot-by-eight-foot cell after being recaptured on my last escape, I started to take a really hard look at myself and what my life was like. I was at the bottom of the pit. I didn't like myself very much at all. I knew that drugs had brought me to this point in life, and I also knew that I would make a change somehow. I had gone as low as you can go.

I took a moral inventory of my actions, and the pain that I caused the people that I cared about. From that time on it has been uphill. I'm still sitting in that same cell, but I no longer blame anyone for it. I put myself in this position, and I will live with it. I still have bad days when I want to escape through a drug-induced haze, but I pick up a book and learn something new or write a letter, anything of a positive nature. I don't have the answers by a long shot, so I just take it one day at a time and thank God for getting me through one more day.

◆

Lionel F., Louisiana State Penitentiary, Louisiana
2 life sentences

March 30

I'VE BEEN IN prison a total of 12 years on a drug conviction.

I still have hope that something will happen in the future and I'll be set free. From that thought I ask myself, "Will I be able to handle that big step when it comes?" Who knows? All I can say is, I'll go on taking life one day at a time. I do know this much, brothers and sisters, drug abuse is not the answer to our problems. Try taking a long look within before you reach that point of no return.

It is my hope that something I have said here may touch you in a way that would stop you from destroying your life, as I have mine.

◆

Lionel F., Louisiana State Penitentiary, Louisiana
2 life sentences

BEING CONFINED IN a maximum-security prison and building relationships is an unheard-of combination. But when I let my defenses down and listened to other people run their stories, I really began to identify with what they were saying. I was amazed to know that we felt the same way, and had been through the same things.

Recovery can work because many incarcerated people share the same hurts, pain, and addictions. When I hear other convicts talking honestly about their past, I forget that we are convicts and I see them as real people with real problems. This helps me build up my courage and also helps strengthen my self-esteem.

The longer I stay in recovery, the easier it is to deal with being in prison, I owe my life to recovery and my Higher Power. I enjoy being clean and sober and being a good person. And I'm building relationships that will sustain me in recovery.

◆

William M., St. Clair Correctional Facility, Alabama
Attempted murder
Life without parole

APRIL 1

I WAS IMPRISONED at age 16. Adjusting to the prison experience as a young substance abuser has been the most difficult and challenging trial of my life. Immaturity quickly became my biggest enemy. Because of youthful ignorance, I aggressively rebelled against the system I blamed for my problems. Consequently, I was labeled an incessant disciplinary problem and prison administrators confined me indefinitely to a six-by-eight segregated cell, where I have remained the last seven years.

In the beginning, despair engulfed me like a noxious haze. There was no meaning to life. Rejected by society and, finally, by the prison where I had been ostracized, I was forced to dig deep within the core of my being to find out what was there. My innards were screaming for attention, for help, but I had no voice with which to intelligently articulate those needs.

Drugs and alcohol no longer were available to block out my pain. Forced to face reality, I was compelled to ask myself the question that would radically change my life: "What, after all your years of incarceration, will you have to show for your time?" To receive help, I reasoned, I first had to begin helping myself.

I began taking responsibility for my actions. No longer do I blame others for my situation. I see life in a new and positive light. I take life one day at a time.

◆

Michael S., Louisiana State Penitentiary, Louisiana
Forcible rape
30 years

I HAVE LEARNED that life is a continuing challenge, not something which I can, on any given day, take for granted. And my biggest challenges are yet to come. I live for the day when I am released from prison, and I can go to the office of the juvenile court, plop my college degree down on the desk, and say, "Just a child when arrested, I spent years in prison. The system gave up on me as an emotionally unstable, chemically dependent adolescent.

"But I didn't give up on myself. Against all odds, I overcame my adversity and went on to college to earn this degree. I now wish to dedicate the rest of *my* life to helping kids in trouble with the law, to create a support system designed to raise their self-esteem and give them hope for the future — to help spare them my journey through hell. Will you help me?"

Because first, I helped myself.

◆

Michael S., Louisiana State Penitentiary, Louisiana
Forcible rape
30 years

April 3

My story is like that of most other substance abusers. But one difference is that — in recovery — I found a Higher Power to relate to, who carried me out of the trap of drug and alcohol abuse to a life of spirituality. In spite of my incarceration, I have remained clean and sober. There are those in prison who are still abusing drugs, but I know that the end results of such abuse can only lead to further incarceration, and even death.

Through God, I have come to understand how frail we are. All my drug-addict friends in the free world are dead now as a result of substance abuse. I find the peace in life that I thought was in drugs and alcohol.

Today I am a positive force in this prison community. As a recycled human being, I spend my time doing constructive things. There are men here who need help, who need role models. Whatever we do, wherever we are, we can help to shape people's lives.

You and I have the responsibility to give something back for all we took by breaking the chain that binds us together as one. When we broke that chain, it caused others to fumble. Our family could not become all they were put here to become because we became a problem to them. We became a broken link in society, therefore, depriving them of our link to a better world. We can give back now, right where we are.

Andrew J., Louisiana State Penitentiary, Louisiana
Murder
Life

STEP ONE: WE admitted we were powerless over alcohol — that our lives had become unmanageable.

Yes, I guess this is all right for those old winos who get locked up every once in a while and don't stay too long in jail. But that didn't apply to me. And how about that home brew I had last week and had to go to the hole for? Aw, that don't count, I thought. I mean, hey, I like to take a drink when I can get it. I guess I'd like to just get drunk and try to forget this place.

Man, I'm just going to have to admit that I can't handle the booze at all. As I look back, I can see that every time I really did any heavy drinking I'd wind up in some sort of trouble. Look where I'm at — and with a life sentence. I'd better get real with myself. Any time alcohol comes near me, I've got to get as much of it as I can, because I don't know when I'm going to get any more.

As I look back, I can say, Yes, I'm powerless over alcohol. My life had become totally unmanageable.

◆

Lawrence J., Louisiana State Penitentiary, Louisiana
Aggravated rape
Life

APRIL 5

I CAME TO prison 21 years ago, and since that time, I've spent only eight months as a free person.

I came to prison with an attitude. I resented authority. I hated being told what to do and when to do it, and the consequences of not complying.

Drugs were easily obtained. Most of the prisoners used them as a solution to maintain their sanity and deal with the stress of confinement. Using it was our way to beat the system and build "easy time." Our view was that they could imprison our bodies, but not our minds.

We were right; we did that by ourselves. We developed a dependency on those drugs that locked our potential abilities inside a psychological prison with a stronger grip than bars and fences could ever hold.

When I first decided drugs had caused enough misery in my life, I doubted my ability to quit. It was then that I realized just how much control my habit had on my life. It told me what to do and when to do it. Yes, I had placed myself under the exact circumstances I was so resentful of in the beginning.

I am not yet fully recovered, but I know what I don't want out of life and will use it as a guide to what can only get better.

◆

Phillip W., St. Clair Correctional Facility, Alabama
Murder
30 years

I'M 21 YEARS old, and I've been in prison a little over two years now. I came from a broken home. My stepfather wanted my mother, but not her kids. When I was 13, I started using drugs because all my friends did, and since I felt left out at home, I didn't want to risk losing my relationships with them, too. As I grew older, my habits grew bigger and eventually led me to commit the crimes I'm now being punished for.

I'd never considered the effect my teenage years had on my addiction, but now that I'm in treatment, I've had to discuss my childhood. I now understand the negative emotions my alcoholic stepfather expressed toward me and how it influenced my behavior.

I look back at my crimes, which were only non-violent burglaries, and realize it wasn't money I was after, it was acceptance. And drugs weren't the solution, they only placed me in the situation of losing the people I cared about. Then I was carried away in chains to a place filled with people who didn't care for each other.

I got into a recovery program to rid my life of bad habits, never contemplating to find the quality that was missing from my life. Here I've found emotions are expressed openly in groups, and problems are shared and resolved when possible. I've felt a welcoming part of the program that will help me develop a productive life.

◆

Charlie S., St. Clair Correctional Facility, Alabama
Burglary, Escape
Life

April 7

I'M A RECOVERING drug addict. I'm also a repeat offender. During my first imprisonment I didn't seek help for my addiction. I've always had my own way of thinking, and sure enough, I figured that time would help my addiction. But I was wrong. The evidence speaks for itself.

I did not seek help because of shame, guilt, and fear of what others would think of me. My pride and reputation kept me from acknowledging to others that I was a crack cocaine addict. When I was released from prison, I began to use drugs more than ever. I always thought that drugs were the problem. But when I returned to prison the second time, I sought help in a treatment program.

I'm a firm believer that without acknowledging my problems to others and God, and trying to deal effectively with past experiences, my life will never be complete. Prayer to my Higher Power and acceptance of my wrongs will surely mean a start on the road of recovery.

◆

Eric H., St. Clair Correctional Facility, Alabama
Robbery
25 years

MY BELIEF IN God is the foundation of my recovery. Without my spiritual foundation, I have no recovery program. Without my spirituality, I tend to focus on release dates, guard towers, razor wire, and bad food.

With my Higher Power working in my life, I tend to focus on the sunset, sunrise, flowers, trees, and the beauty of life. Such a refreshing way of life after the years I have lived in the darkness of addiction and hate. This same freedom from addiction is free for the taking for anyone who is willing to be honest.

◆

Rannie C., St. Clair Correctional Facility, Alabama
Murder
45 years

APRIL 9

I CAME TO prison in 1962 at the age of 23 for robbery, trying to get money for drugs. And drugs have kept me in prison for 30 years — all but 79 days. I have come to find out who I am, and I don't like who I see. At the age of 54, I see myself as a sick person who needs a lot of help.

To stay in recovery each day, I know I need people to help me. I can't do it alone. So I trust the groups here in treatment, and I can talk about my feelings in each one of them. Groups are the backbone of treatment here. We have three different types: support group, social group, and encounter group. We must be honest with group members in order to deal with the things in life and recovery from using drugs.

Thank God that we can receive help at any age if we want it. It's not what we give in life, it's what we do with what we get in life.

I refuse to give up. I know that recovery is a lifetime job, but I am beginning to really see who I am and who I want to be.

◆

William B., St. Clair Correctional Facility, Alabama
Robbery, drug charges
Life without parole

MY EXPERIENCES IN recovery have not been easy. I was confronted by so-called friends at first, saying that I was weak and I "done got soft." As time went on, they stopped making jokes and respected me more for trying to do something for myself.

In recovery I'm dealing with serious issues and feelings. I used to stuff my feelings by using drugs or alcohol. I was kind of scared to face them at first, but now it's almost a daily thing. In my life I don't ever recall showing remorse. Now I feel things like that, and I think about the suffering and hurt that I brought to others.

Recovery has become important to me because I'm young and don't ever want to be confined again. I got another chance at making it. I think recovery will enhance my chances at becoming a better role model in society.

◆

Carmece H., St. Clair Correctional Facility, Alabama
Murder, Attempted murder

APRIL 11

IT IS VERY difficult for me to say much on recovery because I have not been in the program long. But in the short time I have been here, I have come to realize that if we look at the positive things that happen to us, instead of concentrating on the negatives, we will be a better person for it.

Before coming into the program I heard so many negative things about it that I was really reluctant to try it. But now that I'm here, I'm not only glad that I came, but I wish I had done it sooner. It's not just that I want to be here, because I do. The main reason I'm in treatment is that I desperately need it. I know that if I'm not strong enough to make it through this program, I won't be strong enough to make it in society. It was a very difficult decision for me to come to the program, but with every passing day, I realize that I made the right choice.

◆

Joseph R., St. Clair Correctional Facility, Alabama
Robbery
Life without parole

I'VE ALWAYS BEEN afraid to show any love to the people who loved me. I was afraid of being hurt, but by living that way, I've lost the people I loved the most — my family and my wife.

When I started in recovery, I wanted to find out why I was like this. At first, it was very painful to tell some of the things I had done to keep from showing love, but now I can talk about them and try to repair the damage I caused.

I never knew love until now. Love and caring are something special and should be cherished. I pray that my wife will again talk to me so I can try and show her I do care and let her know I'm changing my life.

◆

Dale B., St. Clair Correctional Facility, Alabama
Burglary, Theft, Escape
10 years

APRIL 13

ONE OF MY many character defects is that I want people to do things how and when I want them. When I was out there using, this had great significance for me. If things didn't go the way I thought they should, I'd let this defect basically control my feelings. More than once I ended up drunk over it.

In recovery, I've learned that I have no control over what people do (or don't do) or what they say. Knowing this takes a great burden off of me. I don't sit around worried or angry because of other people's actions. I've also realized that I have more time to spend on helping myself when I'm not worried about others.

Today I try to stay focused on what I need to do. I don't let others control my emotions. If I focus on myself, I feel as if I have more control over myself. And that could save me from a relapse.

◆

Lisa H., Dwight Correctional Facility, Illinois
Burglary
3 years

THERE WAS ABSOLUTE chaos during my active addiction. Starting with broken family ties and loss of jobs, I worked my way up to health problems, disregard for other people, and a reckless lifestyle. I always felt I had my drug use under control. Better yet, I considered myself a functional addict. Even though society is much against this method of altering our moods and although drug abuse is dangerous to our health and state of mind, thousands of addicts still engage in drug use and abuse.

I now realize the dangers of drug abuse, and I have made a choice not to use anymore. At first, drug use was enjoyable, but the joy has disappeared and it is time to reconsider my objectives in life as opposed to wasting myself.

Through the recovery process, I am beginning to learn about the results of my past actions and present drug addiction, as well as about who I can become. Now I have made a choice to accept and face the opportunities as well as the challenges that lie ahead with a clear, unclouded vision, and to make the best of any situation no matter how dark it may appear. I am choosing to do this today, and I will try to live the rest of my life with a sober mind.

◆

Irene C., Dwight Correctional Facility, Illinois
Theft
17 months

April 15

WHEN I TRY to figure out exactly what it was that caused me to be so dependent on alcohol, I can sum it up in one word —escape!

I have had a lot of time to think lately, and I've used this time wisely. I've come to realize that I've been attempting to escape from almost every aspect of my life. I've used alcohol to take away the pain and sorrow I experienced. I realize now that the more I drank, the more pain and sorrow I caused.

During my incarceration, I'm learning other, less painful, ways to cope with the events that are thrust upon me. I use the "Serenity Prayer" at least 25 times a day, saying it over and over in my mind when the need arises. I've come to understand that I have no control over anyone but myself, and no control over most events. I have learned that acceptance can overtake the desire to escape, and courage can change my entire way of living.

Once I began to make the changes I felt were necessary for me, everything else seemed much easier. I try not to dwell on events I have no control over and to accept them with as little irritation as possible. Removing this load of unnecessary baggage gives me more time to concentrate on the things I can improve upon.

◆

Laura R., Dwight Correctional Facility, Illinois
Involuntary death; failure to report
2½ years

I HAVE BEEN to prison three times because of my addiction. I'm willing to accept this now and know that prison and addiction run hand in hand. Acceptance is the biggest part of my recovery.

Every day we have to accept situations that may occur in our lives. To stay clean and sober, we addicts need to accept that we are truly addicts. If we keep this up front every day, we will succeed.

Acceptance can also be about loving ourselves and accepting the way we used to be. Once we start loving ourselves, we will be able to love the people and things around us. Could you imagine how much hatred we must have had for ourselves to inject, drink, or inhale drugs into our bodies? Let's start accepting and loving ourselves today.

◆

Tina B., Dwight Correctional Facility, Illinois
Retail theft
2½ years

APRIL 17

STEP THREE: MADE a decision to turn our will and our lives over to the care of God *as we understood Him.*

In taking my Third Step, it was important for me to consider my will. In prison, it is easy to say I have turned my will over to God's care. But what will I do once I am free from confinement?

I know that I have had enough. I don't want to use again, and I will not use again because the consequences outweigh the high. I want to regain the good pleasurable things of life, including a strong spiritual base on which to stand.

The times I have allowed God to care for me, He has faithfully directed my path. After many tries, I have decided to recommit my life over to the care of God. It is not God's will for men to be prisoners, but He allows certain circumstances to develop in order to perfect His will in our lives.

The program saying, "Thy will, not mine, be done," always helps me to remember Step Three.

◆

Julian B., Cook County Jail, Illinois
Burglary
1 year

NEVER IN MY wildest dreams would I have said, "Hi, my name is Linda and I'm an alcoholic and an addict." Admit it? I couldn't even accept it.

Now I *know* that I am an addict and my life is unmanageable. I realize that acceptance is the answer to all of my problems. Once I accepted my addiction, I was able to get some structure back into my life. There has to be a Power greater than myself that can restore my sanity.

Being in treatment has taught me that I will be an alcoholic and an addict for the rest of my life. However, I do have a choice today — I choose not to use.

◆

Linda H., Dwight Correctional Facility, Illinois
Prostitution
9 months

April 19

WHAT NEED IS there to condemn ourselves? Why kill our spiritual vision? There are many beautiful things in the world that we can touch and contemplate without fear of burning or hurting ourselves.

A good book can soften and enrich us. Nature gives us life. Our spirituality gives us liberty and guides us in the eternal way.

Forget drugs and alcohol. Let's drink pure water and purify ourselves. Let's drug ourselves with light and love and live life in all its splendor. Let's not condemn ourselves.

The great barrier that obstructs our future is in our conscience. The day that we are able to break through that barrier, we will be able to achieve and produce many beautiful things.

◆

Maximo G., Cook County Jail, Illinois
Possession of a controlled substance and weapon
1 year

I AM A 42-year-old addict. This is my third time in the penitentiary. I have spent time in three different drug treatment programs. Each time I relapsed and went right back to drugs.

Relapse is a serious issue for all addicts. We may tell ourselves we can handle it. Some die trying to prove they can handle using drugs. If you are faced with this problem, you are no different from the next addict. If you are someone like me who needs help, reach out to your Higher Power for that help. Recovery is possible; we can learn to live drug-free. Once we admit we have a drug problem, we open doors to recovery. We need to go to meetings and surround ourselves with recovering addicts. We cannot afford to be around people who are using drugs.

We can't use, no matter what. We must go to an A.A. or N.A. meeting the very first day we are released from prison. No matter how much better our lives have become, no matter what the extent of our spiritual healing, we are still addicts. Our disease waits patiently, ready to spring the trap if we give it the opportunity.

Each day, let's carry the principles of recovery into all we do, and each night, let's thank our Higher Power for another day of sobriety. May your Higher Power be with you always.

Bobby H., Staunton Correctional Center, Virginia
Sale of narcotics
8 years

APRIL 21

EVERYONE WHO COMES into A.A. knows from bitter experience that he or she can't drink. I know that drinking has been the cause of all my major troubles or has made them worse. Now that I have found a way out, I will hang on to A.A. with both hands. St. Paul said that nothing in the world — neither powers nor principalities, life nor death — could separate him from the love of God. Likewise, once I have given my drinking problem to God, nothing in the world can separate me from my sobriety.

I know that my new life will not be immune from difficulties, but I will have peace even in times of trouble. I know that serenity is the result of faithful and trusting acceptance of God's will.

I pray that I may welcome difficulties. I pray that they may test my strength and build my character.

◆

Larry D., Staunton Correctional Center, Virginia
Breaking and entering
10 years

I FIRST BECAME involved with Narcotics Anonymous in 1991. At 34, I was sentenced to five years on my first drug charge, but the time was deferred and I was placed in a program that worked hand in hand with Narcotics Anonymous. This is where I really became aware of my spirituality. I learned a lot about the N.A. program, my Higher Power, and faith. I was clean for nine months with this newfound knowledge, but my downfall came when, like a lot of addicts, I thought I had the answer and no longer needed as many meetings. So I slipped. And here I am, incarcerated again.

Now is the time to put together a format for my life to last forever. This means faith in myself to follow this spiritual program, and faith that my Higher Power will work in my life to instill in me the values of recovery. One addict helping another and faith in a Higher Power makes Narcotics Anonymous the greatest possible chance for me to lead a normal life.

◆

Anderson C., Staunton Correctional Center, Virginia
Possession of cocaine
6½ years

APRIL 23

WHAT IT TOOK for me to get clean and sober was going to the penitentiary, doing time, and finding out what I needed to do to change. I found out that it wasn't that hard, if I took just a little time to find out.

Time can help me or hurt me. It took time to elevate myself, but I did it. Knowing what time can offer, if it is used in a positive way, is very important. The goal in all of this for me is being challenged and having confidence in myself — knowing that I can do anything *if I take my time*.

I have a goal in my life which I'm trying to accomplish. I am asking for help, and trying not to be offensive in doing it. Sometimes things seem all mixed up and confusing. But in time (there's that word again), everything will be okay.

◆

Kendrick H., Staunton Correctional Center, Virginia
Robbery
16 years

I BELIEVE THAT the two most difficult emotions we are confronted with from very early in life are fear and anger.

These two emotions are part of our makeup. But in our society, which places a high value on one's ability to wear a mask of false bravado and joviality, these emotions are downright unacceptable.

When we seek to conform to the dictates of society, we unconsciously suppress our fear and anger. By doing so, many of us deal with these internalized pressures by turning to drugs and alcohol.

To recover, we must accept, acknowledge, and deal with the full range of emotions that contribute to a full and wholesome personality. Until we stop denying who we are, where we are, and how we got there, we can't change. We need to address our fears and anger, so we may channel the ensuing energy into pursuits that will benefit us all.

◆

Ronnie G., Nottoway Correctional Center, Virginia
Second-degree homicide
9 years

April 25

LIKE MANY OF you, I don't have many fond memories of growing up. There was so much anger and violence and hatred — and so little caring, acceptance, and love.

I remember one day, I must have been about six or seven, being just minutes away from receiving yet another whipping for some childish prank I'd pulled. Suddenly, I remembered my older sister had told me that by pleading with Dad and asking his forgiveness, she'd escaped being punished. So, when my father snatched me up by the seat of my trousers, I decided to do the same. And to my great surprise, it worked.

My dad passed away several years later. Although I still have mixed feelings about what I went through, through the relationship I've developed with my Higher Power I'm able to see something of the underlying message my earthly father was trying to teach to me about himself, God, and life.

We all make mistakes in life. And it truly does my heart good to know that there is One whose eyes are always upon me. He sees me when I stumble and fall and make mistakes. It truly does my heart good to know that God will always be there for me. And He is always willing to forgive me if I ask.

◆

Ronnie G., Nottoway Correctional Center, Virginia
Second degree homicide
9 years

DRUGS AND ALCOHOL control us; we don't control them. Those of us who have done time or are currently doing time for crimes related to our drug and alcohol abuse are hard pressed to learn this lesson. Addiction is the root problem for most of us in that if we overcome addiction, we will also overcome our criminal behavior. For repeat drug-related offenders like myself who have struggled and been overwhelmed by the lure of getting high, upon release we always managed to convince ourselves to use. We'd say, "I'll get loaded just this once since I just got out, and I'll straighten my life back out tomorrow."

When we take that first hit, our minds are programmed for the next one, and the next, and on and on, in a vicious cycle of defeat which always ends with prison or death. The threat of relapse is a never-ending battle, one in which we cannot afford to let our guard down. Therefore, the main objective of the addict in recovery is to put some distance between the drug use in the "old life" and abstinence in the "new life."

The process of change begins with self, and the first place to look for a helping hand is at the end of my own arm. I finally found my deliverance and personal stability in the power of God, a treatment program that does not fail.

Victor C., Western Missouri Correctional Center, Missouri
Robbery, Armed criminal action
11 years

April 27

ALL MY FRIENDS are junkies or still do drugs, and it is hard for me to stay away from their ways, even in prison. But drugs are my problem. As long as I stay away from my old friends, I don't think I will ever go back. It is easy to say this, but it is not easy to stay away from old partners and the money that dope brings.

The only thing I can say is how important it is to stay away from all our old friends and the neighborhood when we go home, even though it is hard to dig ourselves out of the ghetto.

To me, education is the best teacher, and I need that to get ahead. If I've learned anything in the drug-awareness program, it is to be aware of all things. I've also learned that drugs are the downfall of my life.

◆

Joe C., Western Missouri Correctional Center, Missouri
Robbery
13 years

I BECAME INCARCERATED on September 24, 1991. That is the day my whole life changed. I immediately started to attend A.A. meetings that were being conducted here, and after about a month I decided to begin the Twelve Step program of recovery. I found myself very apprehensive about this; I was not sure I could give myself up to God, or if I had the right to ask Him to forgive me. As I worked the program, I realized that my life had become unmanageable, but I did have a Higher Power that led me to Step Three.

This was the hardest Step for me to do. But through the help of some people in the group and my sponsor, I was able to give myself to God as I understood Him. I began to wake up each morning with a whole new outlook. It didn't matter that I was incarcerated, I was just happy to be alive.

I was then able to do the next four Steps without any difficulty. But when I found myself at the Eighth Step, I wondered how I could possibly make a list of the people I had harmed. I started on this list and ended up with two full pages. I was able to make amends to some of these people, and I know that some day I will be able to complete it. I continue to work the Steps on a daily basis. They allow me to see what life is really about.

◆

Richard W., Western Missouri Correctional Center, Missouri
Involuntary manslaughter, DUI
7 years

APRIL 29

THE FIRST DAY of my recovery felt like a 48-hour day. It was longer than those that followed because of the added stress I felt, wondering how I could reearn all the respect I had lost due to my addiction. And all in the name of a good time.

On my first day of recovery I looked around at all the faces, knowing very few by name, but sure that all the troubles underneath the frowns were due to substance abuse. As we journey day in and day out, recovery holds one logical viewpoint — and that is the importance of our health.

As an addict, I never regarded honor, respect, or quality of life as characteristics worth striving for, but looking back at my life, I remember times when I was of sound health and character, and I didn't have problems with alcohol.

The Twelve Steps are the basis of my recovery. I work the Steps, but always add the "importance of health" as another part of my recovery. Without health it really doesn't matter if my recovery lasts 15 minutes or 15 years. Living 15 minutes or 15 years more without abuse is the name of the game, but good health contributes to happiness, and happiness contributes to success. Good health has become important to me.

Terrance C., Western Missouri Correctional Center, Missouri
Assault
15 years

WHAT DOES MY Higher Power mean to me and how has He helped me in my recovery? My Higher Power is the source of all my strength. In Him I find the strength to continue on my road of recovery. My hope and faith are all I will ever need to survive the temptations my addiction will throw at me. As each moment passes by, I must continue to keep my mind on all the things that have changed since I came to believe in His power. I utilize that Power to overcome any and all of the frustrating circumstances I go through now and those I will encounter in the free world. It's all about constant prayer and meditation, and keeping up my conscious contact with my Higher Power.

I'm looking forward to that day when I walk out the gate a free man to actively put the strength and power I've received from my Higher Power into a more productive life. Recovery for me is a constant learning and relearning process. The beautiful part is that my relationship with my Higher Power will continue to grow into one that's everlasting. I feel that the only way I will not return to active addiction is to continue this relationship, because as He leads me, He will send others with whom I can share those things necessary to stay clean and sober.

◆

James B., Graham Correctional Center, Illinois
Armed robbery
16 years

MAY 1

BEFORE ENTERING THE program, I strongly resisted spiritual concepts and beliefs. I neither understood spirituality nor felt it had anything to offer me. My longing for the nurturing and caring parent, absent from my childhood, limited my ability to understand the concept of a trusting and loving Higher Power.

Perhaps I felt that my prayers were unanswered. My faith in a Higher Power may have been shattered by my belief that if God exists, it was not a loving God. Often, my low self-esteem created the feeling that I was not worthy of the attention or care of a Higher Power, or that it could even exist.

Now, God is there for me. I pray during the day and know that God can do for me what I could not do for myself. Instead of resisting spiritual concepts and beliefs, I welcome them. They are now a welcome part of my recovery — not a shattered dream. And my self-esteem has changed with it. I am worthy of my Higher Power's love and care.

◆

Dallas T., Gateway Program Graduate, Illinois

MY MENTAL AND physical ills are frequently a result of my being unaware of my fears. These fears became a part of my lifestyle when I lacked faith in myself and a Higher Power, when I felt victimized by life. Learning to deal with my fears in a healthy way was an important part of my recovery process.

I had to accept that I was powerless and acknowledge the unmanageability of my life. I saw that my attempts to hide my limitations had crippled me. Although working the Steps can be painful, the road to recovery can only begin with honest self-confrontation and surrender. Until I did this, my progress toward recovery was hindered.

Admitting my human limitations forms the foundation for working each of the Twelve Steps.

◆

Dallas T., Gateway Program Graduate, Illinois

May 3

THROUGHOUT MY RECOVERY, I had to adjust myself slowly to a new and more positive lifestyle. I was troubled at times, and sometimes I still am. But eventually I learned that self-control is the key issue in the lifestyle change that I am going through.

I didn't know about self-control at the start of my recovery, but I learned more and more as I proceeded through the different stages of recovery. As a matter of fact, the farther I proceeded, the greater my self-control became, and the easier it was to recognize exactly what was ahead of me.

After a while, I could see my whole life was beginning to come together in ways that before I could only dream about. It was showing me how my life could be the best that it's ever been. I've seen the light, and I know that I have to keep growing and keep changing. If I do, I'll make it. If I don't, I'll slip back. And then I'll have no self-control again.

◆

Chris B., Graham Correctional Center, Illinois
Burglary, Unlawful possession of firearm ammunition
6 years

YOU'D THINK THAT after living with myself for so long I would understand the root causes of my shortcomings. Often times I placed the blame on everyone and everything around me, which wasn't good because it kept me from progressing in my recovery.

My abusive drug addiction was not the only problem. In fact, it may have compounded the original problems. Truly, "me, myself, and I" have been my biggest problems. I was unmanageable, ungrateful, unpredictable, and most of all, unbearable. I didn't understand what it meant to be blessed.

After being introduced to the concept of taking a moral inventory of myself, I began to use it. I began learning so much about myself. The more I learned, the easier it became for me to address the problem parts of me. Things such as my inability to cope with day-to-day life, low self-esteem, and lack of tolerance.

I was lost. Thanks to my Higher Power and treatment, today I can truly say that I have been found. I understand those root causes that need to be changed.

◆

Joseph T., Graham Correctional Center, Illinois
Armed robbery
30 years

MAY 5

FOR YEARS I went through life feeling that my situation was hopeless. I had been to prison five different times, and each time I was released I went back to the same lifestyle. I felt the world was my enemy. I spent my whole life pointing fingers and blaming everyone and everything for my mistakes.

Since being in recovery, I have found out that my past problems were the result of my own low self-esteem and insecurity. Recovery has taught me to accept life's ups and downs. It has showed me that making mistakes is part of being human. It has taught me to accept responsibility for my action.

I'm no longer lost in the shuffle. I know things don't always have to turn out badly. I'm not a born loser. I'm important and worthy of happiness. I no longer need drugs and alcohol to get through life. Recovery has taught me to accept life on life's terms, one day at a time.

◆

Michael S., St. Clair Correctional Facility, Alabama
Receiving stolen property
Life

WHEN WE HIT rock bottom, one of the first things we had to figure out was how much of an investment we were willing to make to change our lives. We spent thousands of dollars on feeding our addiction and hiding it, and we eventually ended up in prison. We simply had to ask ourselves how much time and energy we were willing to invest in change.

The second question we had to ask ourselves was, "Are we responsible people?" Undoubtedly our answer was no, because none of us were reliable or trustworthy; our past actions spoke for themselves.

But are we answerable for our actions? Are we accountable? Do we take credit for our actions? Like most addicts, especially those of us in a prison-based treatment program, we are quick to take credit for our positive actions. But, when our actions are seemingly negative, we are slow to admit our wrongs.

To begin to put the puzzle together, we have to use the "I.R.A." of treatment — Investment, Responsibility, Accountability — one won't work without the others.

One expression of the I.R.A. of treatment is participation. In this program we must participate in activities such as groups, seminars, and meetings. In them, we can demonstrate our commitment to this program and show our motivation to change.

Robert M., St. Clair Correctional Facility, Alabama
Murder, Burglary
Life plus 11 years

MAY 7

THE TWELVE STEPS and the A.A. fellowship have turned my life around. Giving my life to my Higher Power has made the turn-around easy.

These two decisions were the hardest ones I've ever made. I was an atheist and a nonbeliever, and I never imagined a life without drugs and alcohol. But A.A. and my Higher Power have taken away the desire to use drugs and alcohol. That truly is a miracle to me, a miracle that anyone can receive if they are willing to work.

It took many years for us to reach bottom, and we won't be relieved of our addictions overnight. The miracle doesn't include removing all temptation. Circumstances in our lives may create temptation. We just have to remember past problems and keep our minds on our goals. It's a one-day-at-a-time program. But the results greatly outweigh the effort. The program, fellowship, and my Higher Power have given my life purpose and meaning.

◆

Chris S., St. Bride's Correctional Center, Virginia
Second-degree homicide
10 years

I DON'T BELIEVE any of us wanted our lives to turn out the way they have. Drugs and alcohol have stripped and robbed us of our hopes and dreams.

The good news is that it's never too late for a fresh start. The A.A. program, fellowship, and belief in a Higher Power enables us to have a happy and meaningful life.

We can't let the spiritual side of the program scare us away. It's vitally important to humble ourselves if we expect to achieve sobriety. We failed by ourselves. So why not give the Higher Power idea a chance. If we really want sobriety, we will try the proven method.

There are many things that accompany sobriety and working the A.A. program. We learn to love and to share. We learn what true fellowship and friendship are, too. By opening our hearts and minds, we receive the gifts that are free to the humble.

◆

Chris S., St. Bride's Correctional Center, Virginia
Second-degree homicide
10 years

May 9

EVERY DAY WE all fall short of some illusion or another. We think things look or seem one way, but in reality, they are totally different.

In the insanity of our addictions, we only wanted to see the instant pleasure or excitement that a quick "fix" brought. We never stopped long enough to take in the reality of abuse we were inflicting, not only on ourselves mentally, physically, emotionally, and spiritually, but on our friends and families as well.

Sure, we saw the many advertisements with the mountains and streams and beautiful aspects of nature which were exquisite to the eye. But focusing on these images was only a justification of our addiction and helped cover up the real pictures of our lives, such as abuse, neglect, addiction, and even prison.

But through this program and its many concepts, we have begun to lift the addictive shields from our eyes and minds. We accept the reality of life, and deal with our problems with a positive attitude.

We have learned that if it looks good to the eye, we must take a second look with our minds to see if it's real.

◆

Robert M., St. Clair Correctional Facility, Alabama
Murder, Burglary
Life plus 11 years

THIS IS MY first time in recovery. My main concern is learning effective ways of dealing with my anger. The thing about this program that helps the most with that is group. Using my group has opened my eyes to how screwed-up my thinking and outlook on life have been.

I always thought that drugs were the reason that I resorted to violence. Everything in my prison file is violence-related. That violence is the result of my not dealing with my feelings effectively. In the past I'd use drugs to numb or medicate my feelings, but that only helped until the effects of the drug wore off. Now I talk about painful things from my past and receive input from other group members. Anytime something causes me emotional pain, I kick it around in my group.

We also have seminars here by staff members. Every time I attend, I get more in touch with painful childhood experiences. By talking about them in my group, I find that even though I have these problems, there are always solutions.

For me, the group is my Higher Power. I'm searching for spirituality now, but I'm unsure. I'm working a tight program, so I believe in time I'll get a balance in my life, including spirituality.

◆

Gary P., St. Clair Correctional Facility, Alabama
Attempted murder
15 years

MAY 11

I'VE BEEN IN the program at St. Clair for six months. The greatest thing that has helped me is the group process. I've learned to confront people and not let little things build up inside of me. The best way for me to deal with my feelings is to get them out and talk about them.

Sometimes it's tough, but I always remember that when I feel confused, I'm actually growing in recovery. I must learn not to let things that I have no control over bother me. Change is always to come.

Recovery has brought my family closer together also.

◆

Kenneth P., St. Clair Correctional Facility, Alabama
Theft, Escape
11 years

TRUTH KNOWS NO boundaries. I have found this to be one of the most important truths that I have accepted in recovery. As a sex addict and a sex offender, I was in a big state of denial. I had to face a lot of truth before I could even begin my recovery. And I will have to face the truth for the rest of my life in order to stay in recovery, because once I start telling lies and running from the truth about myself and the things that I've done, I might do them again. Without honesty, I most probably will do them again because one lie leads to another, and then you lose all moral values.

I can't face people every day if I'm not honest with them and myself. Once I got honest with myself, the rest was easy.

◆

Paul S., St. Clair Correctional Facility, Alabama
Sexual abuse, Burglary, Theft
15 years

MAY 13

THE PHILOSOPHY OF St. Clair's treatment program is, "We have awakened and realized that where we are in our lives is not where we want to be." I came to this realization some time ago as I lay on the hard steel cot listening to the tall tales of wealth and power, smelling the pungent smell of sweat, urine, and blood, an almost tangible odor of human misery. Above all of this was the loud, cold clang of giant steel bars, like the gnaw of some grotesque beast eating away at my soul and my freedom with each indiscriminate close of its mouth.

I wept within, silently masking my pain. Flashing before my eyes were scenes from my childhood: my loving parents, the Christmas tree, my own small children, my wife of only seven days. I wept harder. I knew they loved me, but I had forsaken them and God for the gutter of depravity and self-pity. I was a heroin addict.

The vividness with which I can recall that day, and the pain remembered and relived, are constant reminders of my spiritual awakening. Never before my experience in treatment had crying felt so good. Those simple tears, seemingly pent up forever, opened the doors for me to become the person I'd always wanted to be but didn't know how to be. The program's proven, steady pace — plus my determination and God's wonderful mercy — changed my life.

◆

Brian G., St. Clair Correctional Facility, Alabama
Armed robbery
20 years

MOST MAJOR RELIGIONS and philosophies teach "You reap what you sow" in some form. In prison I hear "You get what your hand calls for," "Karma," and "What goes around comes around."

The odds are that a person in prison or in treatment (and especially in prison and in treatment!) has done some serious wrong to themselves and others somewhere along the road. No doubt there is a certain amount of resentment about being confined, but the cycle of Karma never stops. Unlike many things, it continues while we are confined — it does not wait.

If we are working toward happiness in treatment, being happy along the way is requisite. To stay angry all the time in recovery is a waste of effort. We need to lighten up sometimes, laugh sometimes.

Ultimately, the goal of treatment is stability and some sense of happiness in life.

◆

John S., St. Clair Correctional Facility, Alabama
Murder
Life

May 15

WHILE I WAS in the county jail I rededicated my life to my Higher Power. Ever since, my life has seemed to fall back into place. Every step of my prison life seems to be guided by God's hand. He has kept a bad situation from becoming an impossible one.

In my recovery, my spirituality is the biggest and most important part. I truly do not see how people in prison make it without spirituality. God gives me peace and hope in a place where there is not always a lot of hope.

◆

Timothy J., St. Clair Correctional Facility, Alabama
Robbery
4 years

I CAME FROM more than 20 years of using one drug or another, and I've spent a majority of that time in prison. I never thought or believed I was the problem. Drugs were the problem. I'd get clean and healthy while slammed, and get hope that I could do it better. Eventually the day came when that lie didn't work anymore. I took an honest look at myself and knew the solution was about change within me.

My relief from this is living just for today and letting go of old images and perceptions of myself. Some days I can get lost in the old feelings of failure and loneliness. What works for me then is to admit I'm powerless, admit defeat, and take action to change. My faith in a power greater than myself helps me to know there is a kind, loving, and understanding human being underneath all my negative stuff. To get there I need to be honest. I focus on what my Higher Power intended for me. If I'm practicing the Steps of N.A., then I'm living according to God's will and there's hope for me.

My days in prison aren't all good, but they're not all bad. I'm getting to know myself, and I'm doing the footwork to change me — not my addiction. I wake up grateful to be clean, which gives me hope. And I'm truly grateful there is a program of recovery.

◆

Kathryn N., California Institution for Women, California
Petty theft with prior
16 months

MAY 17

TO BECOME READY to change, I practice willingness and open myself to the possibility of change. I realize there are defects that hinder my usefulness in my program and toward others, but I need only to surrender my old ways to God.

I no longer fight, nor do I try to control others. I simply believe that with God's help, I am changed. Affirming this belief makes me full of awareness, light, and love, and helps me to face each day with hope.

I'm working my program because it's helping me to remember that I am striving for a better way and a new outlook on life. Since I have been in treatment, a lot of my old ways of thinking have been toned down or eliminated. In group I can talk out my problems. Once I'm willing to name my defects and claim them as my own, I can discard them just for that day.

As I grow in the program, many of my defects become more objectionable to me than they previously had been. I need to keep an open mind and heart, so that I can become happier with myself and maintain my serenity. I have reviewed my life and what I have done, and I am willing for God to remove all my defects of character. I have asked for help because I want to live a life of sobriety and let go of my old self. Each new day, I must determine if I am truly ready to change my life.

Frank S., St. Clair Correctional Facility, Alabama
Possession of a controlled substance
25 years

WHEN I WAS first incarcerated, I had a lot of destructive anger stuffed inside me, anger I've been stuffing my entire life. When I'm angry, I tend to put up a front by laughing and joking. I also turned to alcohol and drugs in order to cope.

I have learned in my recovery that I need to turn my destructive anger into constructive anger. In order to do this, I have to start talking about the things and people that make me angry. That way my anger won't get built up inside of me. This will also help me to build relationships, which is something that I could not do before.

I never realized that it was anger that was the root of my alcohol and drug addiction. I had always blamed it on other people and situations. Now that I know what the real problem is, I can take the necessary steps in order to control and confront my anger, which in turn will help me to continue on course in my recovery.

◆

Mike H., St. Clair Correctional Facility, Alabama
Rape
15 years

May 19

IN MY OPINION, self-love is very important in recovery. I need it in order to get away from drugs or whatever it is that's hindering me from a normal and prosperous life. Self-love brings about self-respect. If I care about myself, I'll take better care of myself. When on drugs or alcohol, I stop caring about myself and others around me.

When I was on drugs, I didn't care about myself or how others saw me. All that mattered to me was another hit. And after it was gone, another one after that, and on and on. The program has taught me how self-love plays a role in recovery. I know now that if I love something, I will take care of it. That includes me. Drugs destroy my body. So, I plan to keep a healthy body.

Another important issue in recovery is goals. I once was completely lost. No goals. The program taught me to set goals in life, so one day I could get out of prison a drug-free man and obtain a job. I want to accomplish something in life. But it's impossible to have anything and be a drug addict.

I was once lost, but through the help of God and treatment, I'm slowly coming back to reality. Drugs aren't the way. And I'm discovering how to love myself more, to set goals in life, and to go after those goals. And to never give up on myself.

◆

George S., St. Clair Correctional Facility, Alabama
Theft of property
17 years

I'M 31 YEARS old and I've been locked up more or less all my life — if not in prison and jail, then inside. I left home when I was 13 years old because I got caught stealing money. After that I lived on the streets, and stole, robbed, and did whatever I had to to survive. All along I was searching for something that I couldn't find. I always had it inside me, but it was locked up behind drugs and alcohol for many years.

I hurt the people I loved the most. I had a lot of hate and anger, but I didn't know how to deal with it the right way. To me, the right way was to get drunk, get high, and say, "To hell with it." In doing this, I put myself in prison.

When I came back to prison, I was a very messed-up young man and didn't know what to do except stay wired on mind-altering drugs. Then I heard about the treatment program. Now I'm trying to deal with the pain, the shame, and the things I've done.

I love recovery. It's not easy — it's the hardest thing I've ever done — but I know if I don't change my life, I'll spend it in prison or in a pine box. Remember, hate needs no introduction, only a reason to be provoked. But love, that I have to work on every day. For me, recovery is the only way.

◆

Jeffrey B., St. Clair Correctional Facility, Alabama
Burglary, Theft, Escape
10 years

May 21

SINCE COMING INTO recovery I have learned that I am powerless over my sexual addiction. It will always be an ongoing battle to control my way of thinking, even though I still feel inner pain.

Through years of growing up I became a sick-minded person, a person that hurt many people because of the hurt I'd experienced as a child. Although I felt shameful and guilty sometimes because of my actions, I couldn't stop them.

It means so much to have the help of other recovering addicts who understand what I've been through and who see my desire to change the way I think and feel. I am also thankful that God is there for me and will help me through my struggle.

Coming to prison, having my hopes and dreams shattered, is what it took for me to hit rock bottom and realize just how much I needed a recovery program in order to change my life.

◆

Jeffrey H., St. Clair Correctional Facility, Alabama
Rape
Life

I HAVE GOTTEN in touch with a part of my life I would have never thought existed. Since I've been in recovery, I have learned to love and believe in myself, respect and trust others, to confront and build positive relationships, and to deal with feelings and emotions and have the courage to express them.

Before now I would blame others for my problems, and if I couldn't blame others, I would blame drugs or alcohol. By being in treatment, I see that it goes deeper. All the pain, hurt, resentment, anger, and shame I held inside was brought to the surface just by dealing effectively with my past and learning to recognize and identify what was happening inside of me.

I never thought I would be in prison. I never thought I was a bad person. I never thought I would be punished for my thinking. The road we travel is the road of our choice. I've learned that if I am hurt, angered, sad, or depressed, I need to talk about it.

I'm still on my road to recovery. It's a complicated road to travel, and every obstacle is a challenge. God has given me the will to change, but the choice is still mine. As of now, my life has made a 90-degree turn to a more positive moral plane. I encourage treatment to every one, because the only way out is from within.

◆

Larry M., St. Clair Correctional Facility, Alabama
Rape, Robbery, Kidnapping, Escape
Life without parole

May 23

WHILE WE ARE running rampant on the streets, our minds are clouded by the chemicals that we've consumed. This is what I call incarceration. When we finally get rescued, our minds start to clear. We don't really understand what has happened to us. We start contemplating trying to get some understanding of the situation.

Since I'm a repeat offender, it didn't take long to figure it out. My best thinking had messed me up again.

Recovery has been a long process for me. I've finally come to know and really understand that when I start thinking on my own is when my relapse begins. Today I have a Higher Power who I call God. I ask God to help me through all endeavors. When I start thinking my old thoughts, I ask for His help. He might not give me what I want, but He always gives me what I need. I used to try to figure out what went through my mind before I committed another crime. But now there's no more negative thoughts of waking up in prison trying to figure out what happened. The thoughts that run through my mind today are of the peace that I had yesterday.

◆

Keith T., St. Clair Correctional Facility, Alabama
Burglary
10 years

I GREW UP in a very dysfunctional family. My father was a violent and abusive alcoholic, my parents divorced when I was young, and my world was filled with confusion, abandonment, chaos, and anger.

I was angry and lonely, so I started drinking and using drugs. I had dreams for the future, but I couldn't see any way of reaching them. I was overwhelmed by the helplessness I felt to change the path I was on. Drugs and alcohol became my way of dealing with my pain and anger.

One night, in a moment of drunken, blind rage I shot a man and killed him. I didn't see it coming, but looking back it's easy to see how it came to be. I was sent to prison for 40 years for murder. That made me angrier than ever.

But somewhere along the way I got tired of hating. I turned to God and asked Him to help me. Through God's grace I found a program that helped me start dealing with all the feelings I'd been holding in and running from all my life. I've found the strength and courage to see myself as I really am, to face the problems which led to my addiction. Through the program, I feel I have been released from the anger that drove me down the path of self-destruction.

◆

John D., St. Clair Correctional Facility, Alabama
Manslaughter
30 years

SOBRIETY — WHO NEEDS it? I need it. I'm tired of not feeling alive and not having choices in my life. I never participated in any sort of substance abuse program until now, and it's helping me to realize I have a disease. I always felt I could and would quit drugs on my own, and I felt bad when I couldn't keep my promise. I thought I wasn't strong enough, that if I just had a little more willpower I could do it. But I finally realized I needed help.

I still have fears that I'm trying to deal with: fear of facing the world sober, fear of going back into the working world, fear of being criticized for being an addict and a woman. I'm also afraid of trying to earn the trust and respect of my kids again. And not only my children, but parents, family members, and friends who will, no doubt, feel uneasy about whether I'll make it this time.

It's going to take a long time to mend all the hurt and anger I brought about, but I'm willing to make this sacrifice because I need and really want what my drug abuse made me lose. It's not going to be easy, but with education, taking it one day at a time, and with the support and guidance of my caseworker, sponsor, and other recovering people, I will come out on top. I will hold my head up again. And I will live as I should, forever free from my addiction.

Barbara M., California Institution for Women, California
Petty theft
16 months

IN ORDER TO operate successfully, each of the three parts of recovery must be nourished — spiritual, mental, and physical. We must be nourished spiritually in order to produce and develop faith. Faith is what gives us a fresh mental and spiritual attitude.

The counselors here are an inspiration to me. I listen to everything they say. They are very successful after all they have been through, and they give me hope that I can do it also.

I like myself a lot, and I feel blessed to be a part of this program. When I go home, I know to take one day at a time.

◆

Jean R., California Institution for Women, California
Possession of a controlled substance
3 years

MAY 27

I GUESS YOU could call me a three-time loser, because this is my third time in an institution because of crimes related to drugs. At first I was unaware that my constant drug use was the cause of my coming back to prison. I would always blame someone or something else for my being in a situation that brought me into confinement.

This last trip I heard about the treatment program. I said, "What luck, I'll sign up so that I can be close to home." After arriving here, I decided that I didn't want to be in the program, but I was told either I enter the program or go back North. So here I am. I'm really glad that I stayed because I have gotten a lot out of this program. I started out in denial. I figured I didn't need a program because I didn't sell my body for drugs and I always maintained some kind of job. I had a problem and didn't even know it.

I'm glad that I was able to realize that I was powerless over drugs and that my life had become unmanageable. Now I am on my way to recovery. But in order for me to keep this sobriety I must rely on outside support, group, and my Higher Power.

Today I know that the most important thing to me is me — and staying clean and sober.

◆

Mildred S., California Institution for Women, California
Receiving stolen property
16 months

EVERYONE HAS A certain amount of creativity, but not everyone takes the time to use it. If everyone took just one hour out of their lives to attempt to create something, then this world would be a better place to live. A perfect example is this book.

A few good people took time out of their lives to write a few words on a piece of paper in an attempt to help someone else. The combined creativity of those men and women are in this book. If something that one person wrote helps just one other person, then the time they spent was worthwhile.

Let's not be afraid to create something. Let's share our creativity with others. If you create something, don't keep it to yourself, because the only way to keep what you have is by giving it away.

◆

Rockey S., St. Clair Correctional Facility, Alabama
Child abuse
20 years

"NO FREE LUNCH." What does this house tool mean? To me it means that there is nothing free in the program or in life. Everything that is worth having is worth paying for, and everything in life has a price. If we are not willing to pay the price then we won't get what we want.

After many years, I am finally willing to do what it takes. I am willing to pay the price.

◆

Edward F., St. Clair Correctional Facility, Alabama
Rape

I HAVE AWAKENED and realized that I am powerless over drugs, and I will be in recovery of some type for the rest of my life if I wish to stay sober. In recovery, the group process is a vital part for me. By using my groups, being open, and running my story many times, I get in touch with my true feelings that have been buried deep within me. Once these feelings surface, I start to understand what my issues are and why I have them. I understand myself better now. And by using my groups I'm on the road to recovery.

◆

James H., St. Clair Correctional Facility, Alabama
Murder
Life

MAY 31

I AM GLAD that I have a chance to change my life and to find out more about myself in recovery. The Step that helps me out the most is Step One, admitting my powerlessness. When I feel powerlessness, I know I need to work my program.

This is my first time in recovery. I have been in the program now over two years. I believe in God, and I feel real good about where I'm at.

◆

Michael T., St. Clair Correctional Facility, Alabama
Robbery
Life without parole

WHILE IN THE county jail I hit bottom. I had a nervous breakdown and cut my throat four times. At that time, I knew I didn't want any more drugs. When I came into the system, it still took me a couple of years to get into a treatment program.

I feel that I've gained immensely from this program. I've gotten in touch with many factors leading up to my being incarcerated.

I have recently gotten into the A.A. program. I think anyone who lives up to, and by, the Twelve Steps of A.A., will become a more productive person.

I can't pinpoint any certain subject that has caused my misfortunes in life, and I can't say that any one subject in recovery has been my main issue — I have so many — but I do believe that this program, the groups, and my Higher Power have been most beneficial to me.

◆

James D., St. Clair Correctional Facility, Alabama
Possession of a controlled substance
15 years

JUNE 2

THERE IS A way to overcome this disease of alcoholism. It's called Alcoholics Anonymous. I, as a recovering alcoholic, consider myself living proof.

I am from a family of alcoholics, some of whom are in recovery. My mother was a chronic alcoholic. When her alcoholism worsened, she attempted suicide. Eventually after a few trips to the psych ward, she started attending A.A. As she progressed, I worsened. I'd seen all the attention she received in her drinking days and I wanted it. I went to any length to get it.

My disease progressed from the age of 15 to 18. I was kicked out of eight to ten schools due to my alcoholic behavior. I was constantly fighting, not showing up, or being drunk and disorderly. By the age of 18, I was having daily visits from the local police. In a desperate bid for a drink, I even got in a physical fight with my mother. I left the house, and a police officer pulled in front of me and arrested me for battery. In court, I was full of fear of what might happen. I stood in front of the judge, trembling. He committed me to the Department of Corrections, Juvenile Division. I was devastated. It took more drinking for me to hit bottom, and now I'm back in prison. But I'm in the Gateway program here at Graham and have made extreme progress. There's more to life than drugs and alcohol — my family!

David H., Graham Correctional Center, Illinois
Aggravated battery
4 years

GOD IS MY shield. Between me and all the scorn and indignity in the world is my trust in God. Nothing has the power to penetrate or spoil my inner peace. There is no bond or union on earth to compare with the union between a human soul and God. That oneness of purpose puts me in harmony with God and with others who are trying to do His will. That's why I choose God to be my shield.

◆

James P., Ventress Correctional Facility, Alabama
Robbery
8½ years

JUNE 4

I CAME FROM a one-parent home. Even though I don't blame my shortcomings on that now, I did a few 24 hours ago. I got caught in 20 years of addiction. I felt it was everyone else's fault. I used everything I could think of for my reasons for going in and out of the revolving doors of our so-called system.

Nevertheless, on the outside I kept going into smoke houses like I would find the answer. I used every drug available and ended up in every correctional facility in Illinois. I've slept in abandoned buildings, back seats of cars, trucks, and vans. Today I can admit that it got so bad I found myself eating out of the garbage cans behind stores. There were days when I totally gave up, I didn't know which way to go or what to do. I found myself getting up out of people's doorways looking for that next fix.

You could say I was lost. It took a Power greater than myself for me to even begin to see the light at the end of the tunnel.

◆

Dallas T., Gateway Program Graduate, Illinois

IT'S HARD TO believe after all the treatment I have struggled with, that a word or phrase I use or meditate on daily can keep me sober each day of my life.

My addiction was like a big security blanket. When I was feeling cold from all the trauma in life and didn't know how to meet them head on, I covered myself up with that security blanket called addiction. And I didn't come out until it was okay. But my new lifestyle doesn't require a security blanket. It just requires one day at a time, a Higher Power, balance, and a mirror to look at and tell myself I'm whole and I'm okay.

My new lifestyle gives me more pleasure out of life than that old security blanket called addiction ever did. I've got my Higher Power to thank for that.

◆

Richard E., Moberly Correctional Center, Missouri
Second-degree murder
20 years

JUNE 6

I ENTERED A two-phase substance abuse program that incorporates the Twelve Step program, positive mental attitude, and various techniques to change habits and thinking patterns. The program helped me be honest with myself and with my significant others. Being honest made me realize that I need to surround myself with people who want to remain drug-free. I quit hanging around people who got high or that glorified getting high. The repetition of working my program, which includes daily self-talk, has rid me of old habits related to my drug abuse. A couple of examples are that I have stopped doing things in excess and have significantly decreased procrastinating.

After completing the program, I joined the Narcotics Anonymous group here, which I helped form, so that I could continue to associate with like-minded individuals. Recovering addicts need a support system. There is no shame in needing help and asking for it.

After abusing drugs for approximately 20 years, the hardest thing for me to do was to push my pride and ego aside and admit that I needed help with my life. Once I did that, things began to start falling in place. What picked me up and keeps me up is my Higher Power, working my program daily, and staying true and honest with myself, a recipe I recommend to everyone.

Andrew F., Moberly Correctional Center, Missouri
Sale of a controlled substance
30 years

COMING INTO RECOVERY presented me with several problems. The first was the rebuilding of my self-image. I had portrayed a negative and false image most of my life due to my criminal activities and the negative environment in prison.

Rebuilding my self-image took many hours of intense group therapy. I realized I had to drop my foolish pride and humble myself to others. I had to take labels off myself and others. After I did this, I realized we all had the same goals in life, which is to better ourselves and to live a life free of drugs and alcohol. Those are the keys to a productive life.

To maintain my sobriety, I must be in recovery for the rest of my life, one day at a time.

◆

James C., St. Clair Correctional Facility, Alabama
Robbery
25 years

JUNE 8

WHEN I WAS on the streets I never had any goals. It seems like it took a trip to prison to realize what I really wanted in life.

While on the streets, all I wanted was to have fun. I kept up my image by hurting people in order to maintain the things I had and to get more. I sold drugs, smoked reefer, and drank. But now I realize I not only hurt myself, but also the people who care for and love me.

After I came to prison I thought about my case and how it occurred. I decided I wanted to help prevent others from making mistakes I have made.

Therefore, I've set goals to better myself, change my patterns of behavior, and help kids who are doing things I did at their age. I feel that I can speak of my experiences and get across to kids that partying, violence, and hanging in the streets to impress others isn't going to profit them anything but trouble and problems. I know, because it landed me here with 30 years of prison time.

That's my goal while I'm here and when I get out of prison. Hopefully, I can make a difference.

◆

Winfred F., St. Clair Correctional Facility, Alabama
Attempted murder
30 years

ONE OF THE most important things that I have gotten out of A.A. is not to be ashamed to ask for help.

When someone has a gun pointed at you, you are scared. That's how I feel about my drug habit. Drugs have a gun pointed at me, and it's ready to fire. I'm scared, because I know that if I make the wrong move, the gun will go off.

That's the position I will be in when I get out of prison.

A.A. has taught me that being scared is wise. A.A. will help. I think of A.A. as my bullet-proof vest against drugs as long as I use it properly.

◆

Lester T., Louisiana State Penitentiary, Louisiana
Aggravated burglary

June 10

FOUR WEEKS AGO a friend of mine cut his throat with a razor blade. He lived. Last night a friend of mine hung himself in his cell. He died.

Am I going to end up like them? I used to wonder about it. I even swallowed three razor blades back in 1977. I was so tired of life.

I'm 35 years old, and I am in prison for the fifth time. Drugs and drinking are my downfall, 100 percent. No more for me. Easy to say, but hard to do, right? That's why there is A.A. out there to help me.

A.A. can show us a lot if we listen. There are people in every A.A. group that can relate to us, people who have been through the same things and more.

A.A. and treatment have given me a way out of drugs and drinking and have given me hope for the future. The more I listen, the more help I get. Like they say, the program works *if you work it*.

◆

Lester T., Louisiana State Penitentiary, Louisiana
Aggravated burglary

BOTH PARENTS, BROTHERS, sister, cousins, grandparents, uncles and aunts, all are dead. And on top of that, I'm back in prison again.

I took drugs to cure my loneliness. Well, I guess I succeeded in that, because now I have 5,300 inmates to hang with, but the loneliness is still there. Even after 26 years of drugs, it is still there.

But during A.A. meetings I feel content. I am among people who are also lonely, and who have been down the same road as me. A.A. doesn't bring all my loved ones back, but it stops me from joining them in the graveyard.

◆

Lester T., Louisiana State Penitentiary, Louisiana
Aggravated burglary

JUNE 12

WHILE IN ACTIVE addiction my life was miserable. Most of my time was spent drinking and drugging, trying to escape from my many problems. Of course, that only made them worse.

Then a wonderful thing happened. My problems caught up with me, and I was sent to prison to serve a life sentence. I was lucky that I hadn't killed someone or been killed myself during my addiction. Instead I was given an opportunity to turn my life around.

After coming to prison I entered a drug treatment program where I suddenly found myself surrounded by other addicts just like me who had spent the majority of their lives running from their problems. I wasn't alone after all.

I no longer run from my problems. Now I meet them head on, always looking for the solution that I know is there. Solving problems is a major source of strength for anyone willing to take action.

◆

Kelvin C., St. Clair Correctional Facility, Alabama
Robbery
Life

ANGER AND FEAR blend together so well that I lose sight of just exactly what it is I am feeling. I find myself wanting to act out in anger when I feel afraid of making mistakes, when I'm personally threatened, or when I feel simply unable to cope. I try to recognize my fears and lessen them with positive messages, so I don't waste all my energy on irrational thoughts.

I put this energy to better use by coming up with solutions and considering options so that my anger and fear become secondary. I'm able to cope with certain degrees of anger and fear. It helps me to slow down and give myself a better chance to resolve my feelings.

I don't want to minimize my anger or fear, but I do want to bring them down to a level I can deal with so I can cope with the situation at hand. Then, when I have time, I evaluate exactly what I am feeling and deal with that on a deeper level.

◆

Alan M., St. Clair Correctional Facility, Alabama
Murder
Life

JUNE 14

BEFORE COMING INTO recovery, I did all my own thinking. By doing so, I have committed many wrongs, from stealing to drugging. And I ended up somewhere I didn't wish to be: incarcerated.

Now that I'm in recovery, I have learned that we should sometimes let someone else do the thinking for us. I also see that going through the 18 months of the treatment program is only the beginning of my recovery. If I intend to stay clean and drug-free, I must continue my recovery for the rest of my life. My recovery is due to my Higher Power. Without Him, nothing is possible.

◆

Marvin B., St. Clair Correctional Facility, Alabama
Burglary
15 years

BY BEING CONFINED I came to know a lot about myself. I know that I had a real bad addiction and have had lots of problems. In my life, drugs and alcohol have really made me avoid a lot of my responsibility. I lost all control of myself and just started robbing people. I didn't realize I needed help as badly as I did.

I'm really glad to have another chance to talk about it, because the way I was going, I'm lucky to be here to write this. I pray to my Higher Power all the time because my addiction still talks to me. I pray that I can make it in life and think clearly. A big reason is that I've lost my wife this time. She died and left me with two sons. Now that I'm here, I've got to try and change my old ways because my kids are going to need me in the long run just like they need me now. They are my main reason for my not wanting to let my addiction talk to me and keep me put away for the rest of my life.

Recovering is my goal, so that I can see once again. I want to come out of the darkness and back into the light and be all that I can — for myself and my kids.

◆

Harry R., St. Clair Correctional Facility, Alabama
Robbery
4 years

JUNE 16

I WAS IRRESPONSIBLE, so they sent me to a place where I had no responsibilities. I wasn't a productive member of the community, so they isolated me from the community. I wasn't positive and constructive, so they put me in a place where we're degraded and made useless. I wasn't trustworthy, so they put me where there is no trust. I wasn't kind, so they placed me where I was subjected to hatred and cruelty. I wasn't loving, so they put me where there was little love.

They wanted me to be nonviolent, so they placed me where there is violence all around. They wanted me to quit being a tough guy, so they placed me where the tough guy is respected. They wanted me to be a winner, so they placed me where all the losers are housed under one roof. They wanted me to quit exploiting people, so they put me where people exploit one another.

They wanted me to see myself, and when I looked around, I didn't like what I saw. I wanted to change what I was. Now they're helping me to do that.

◆

Walter C., St. Clair Correctional Facility, Alabama
Murder
Life

JUNE 17

IN THE PROGRAM, I've learned about succeeding and achieving my goals. A goal is a purpose I commit myself to totally. In order to achieve it, I must motivate myself consistently. I move toward my goals by being in the program where I'm surrounded by individuals who are thinking of constructive and positive things. That way, I won't be led in the wrong direction.

◆

Wallace R., St. Clair Correctional Facility, Alabama
Burglary
65 years

FIRST OF ALL, I want to acknowledge my Higher Power. Without Him in my life, I couldn't be honest, I couldn't trust people, I couldn't forgive people. My Higher Power has given me the courage to face my infirmities. Before, I was lost. I hated my life. I hated myself. But now all that has gone away.

I'm a recovering drug addict/alcoholic. Through the help of the program here, I'm a lot better today than I was 45 days ago. The program and the knowledge and experience of the counselors have helped me to understand my reasons for doing drugs and my problems with anger and depression.

I hope one day I can help others to recover. My approach will be what I've learned in program, but most importantly, God's way. I will, through God's wisdom, show others the importance that spirituality plays in everyday life. I will challenge others to try it God's way since their way doesn't work, just like my way didn't work.

Spirituality teaches us wisdom. It teaches us patience. It helps us to fight off anger and depression. It helps us not to do drugs and alcohol. It offers another way of life.

◆

Henry T., St. Clair Correctional Facility, Alabama
Attempted murder
25 years

I'M 38 YEARS old, and I've been locked up off and on for 19 years or so. But three months of recovery have done wonders for me, and gave the word "change" new meaning. You see, drugs and alcohol were always the downfall in my life. After three months in treatment, I quit and moved back out into the negative part of prison with all my old friends and the dope. But I didn't want to get high. After a few days of turning offers to get high down, the dopers started to stay away from me.

Well, after all the years I didn't fit in, I'm finally clean! I took a urine test, and I think even the officer was surprised. My goals are to be a better person and stay clean. I know how to work an N.A. and A.A. program now. I also know I'll be in recovery for the rest of my life, and I'll always be wanting to help others.

I thank God each day for all the blessings and the power to make things better.

◆

Ricky M., St. Clair Correctional Facility, Alabama
Robbery, Drugs, Escape
Life plus 17 years

June 20

AFTER SEVERAL DAYS of being doped up, I came to my senses in jail. My first thought was, "What have I done?" This was probably the best question I've ever asked, because God showed me what I did, why I did it, and what I had to do to make things right.

Since then, I've overcome three life sentences, and God was behind it. It's through His love and grace that I'm able to write these words. I find victory in God. When my mind starts to wander off in negative thoughts, I call into remembrance the words of God, and this helps me to overcome my negativity.

I realize that I'll never be cured, but with the help of God, I'll never get sick again.

◆

LaBarron D., St. Clair Correctional Facility, Alabama
Robbery
20 years

WE BUILD OUR own environment. I know there are times when we doubt that our present state of being is of our own construction, but if we can open our minds to the truth then we'll be one step closer to change. The truth can bring great possibilities, if we will only look for it.

I write these thoughts down because I, too, forget that I'm responsible for my life.

I need to become attuned with my emotions and feelings. I must be who I truly am, and not what or who others want me to be. I am human, and I will find my true self when I feel love for myself and learn to forgive myself. When I find my true self, I will be fulfilled and not desire to fill the void with drugs or alcohol. One day I will be in that void with all of my true feelings. Then I will be me.

◆

John J., St. Clair Correctional Facility, Alabama
Armed robbery
20 years

JUNE 22

BEFORE I CAN attack my drug problem or my problems in general, I must first understand why I do what I do. How did I end up this way? What is it that caused my life to be in such a devastated state?

In my case, I know it's crack cocaine. I know how I started. I'm in the process of knowing why as well as how to demolish my addiction to this lethal drug. But this drug is very powerful, and to try to fight it alone is useless. I have come to realize the importance of believing in a spiritual being to help me overcome my addiction.

Man's tactics will never win the war on drugs. We need a Power far greater than man. We need the power of God. If we develop a spiritual side, we will no doubt win this war on drugs. By having a spiritual side, we will have love, courage, faith, commitment, acceptance, patience, self-respect, honesty, confidence, trust, and hope. The knowledge of these alone is powerful against the war on drugs. A person with a spiritual background acts, thinks, feels, and carries himself differently than a person who relies solely on himself. With all that on our side, how can we possibly go wrong?

◆

George L., St. Clair Correctional Facility, Alabama
Robbery
5 years

THIS PROGRAM HAS given me the tools to maintain a drug-free lifestyle. It's not going to be easy, but I know putting forth the effort will help me to accomplish the goals that I have set.

I need drugs and alcohol to medicate my emotional pain. Drugs and alcohol aren't my problem, but only a symptom of my greater problems. I have to develop a new outlook toward myself, others, and life so I can be a more responsible and productive citizen of the world.

To me, sacrifice is a key element. I must sacrifice my addiction to change my life. To be a success, to have sobriety, and to feel good about myself, I must make many sacrifices in my life. Eventually, my sacrifices will help make up my recovery.

◆

Bobby M., St. Clair Correctional Facility, Alabama
Rape, Burglary
Life without parole

JUNE 24

WE ALL WANT good results from life: in our homes, our work, and in our contacts with other people. The single most important factor to guarantee good results, day in and day out, is a healthy attitude.

Our attitude is something we can control. All the people in our world will reflect back to us the attitude we present to them. Our attitude toward life determines life's attitude toward us. The environment can only return to us a corresponding effect, that's why we determine the quality of our own life. We get back what we put out.

As soon as a person begins to change, his surroundings will change. People with good attitudes have one thing in common, they expect more good out of life than bad. They expect to succeed more often than fail — and they do.

The world doesn't care if we change; nothing can change until we do. The answer is attitude. The first thing we need to do is mentally become the people we wish to become. And remember, others reflect our attitudes; our environment is a mirror, often a merciless mirror, of ourselves. If we treat everyone with whom we come in contact as the most important person on earth, we'll receive the same treatment.

Douglas D., St. Clair Correctional Facility, Alabama
First degree robbery
99 years

I'M WRITING TO the person who has sexual issues and is afraid to ask for help.

I'm presently in a group with people who have committed sex crimes. I was raped when I was 17 years old. I never really dealt with the problem until I entered this program. At first it was hard to sit and listen to people who had committed sex crimes, but I'm starting to realize that they are sick and begging for help. Sometimes it's hard to understand, but I have to keep an open mind and remember that all of us are sick.

Being in this group has helped me to understand what drives a person to commit a sex crime. I just wish we could have reached them before they committed the crimes. Sexual abuse and sex addiction are hard issues to deal with, but not dealing with them is worse.

◆

Billy T., St. Clair Correctional Facility, Alabama
Armed robbery
40 years

June 26

I HAD PERSONAL experience with my friend the dope man for almost 15 years. The whole time I knew him, he was always there for me.

At one point in my life he had me sell everything I owned, including trying to sell my daughter on the black market. That's how badly I needed him.

Then long about a year ago, the police came to my door and took me first to jail, then to prison. At this point, something made me open my eyes and see that the dope man wasn't my friend.

Then my Higher Power took over my life and became my true friend. My Higher Power will see me through to the end.

◆

Carol T., California Institution for Women, California
Possession, Sales
2 years

MY ALCOHOL AND drug-use disgraced me, and caused my personality to change totally until I became an irresponsible person lacking judgment. The substance made itself the sole object of my love. It caused me to lose respect and recognition from my relatives, friends, and even strangers.

It does not matter to which social circle we belong, because when we are victims of alcohol or drugs, we pass into the circle of the undesirable of society. Many times, we do not realize that we are elements of conflict and confusion, that we are destructive, out of order, and outside of the peace of our own families and those who live in agreement and unity with life.

In the lifestyle of alcohol and drugs, there is something so dark that I can not describe its origin. That is why the Program suggests we find a Power greater than ourselves. Only by looking for help from the highest and divine Power will we be able to survive this crisis that is consuming us.

◆

Maximo G., Cook County Jail, Illinois
Possession of a controlled substance and firearm
2 years

JUNE 28

THIS PROGRAM IS my last chance. Each day in this program is my last chance. Knowing this, I must put forth the effort and strive to make a change in my life.

◆

Bobby M., St. Clair Correctional Facility, Alabama
Rape, Burglary
Life without parole

I'M 31 YEARS old and currently serving my first term in prison. I've been using drugs off and on since I was 13 years old. I've been busted many times for slamming speed and for possession of heroin. I've been to detox centers five times. I lost my husband and kids. I prostituted myself. Each time I got busted I went back out to the streets, knowing full well that when they caught me I was going to prison. Using cost me everything — and I still wasn't ready to stop.

I signed up for this drug program so I would be transferred closer to my friends and family. As if it really mattered — I had alienated myself from my entire family. But in spite of my motives I now feel like I owe my life to this program and what it has done for me. I had been busted for nearly five months before the fog finally started to lift. It's been seven months now, and I'm just now beginning to think clearly.

If I had not come to prison, I'm convinced I would be dead. I live my life now by taking my recovery one day at a time. Recovery is rewarding, but at times it's not easy. God knows I have a long way to go. I have been living His will for me each day instead of my own, and so far it's working for me. I simply realize that everything happens for a reason, and God will help me as long as I'm helping myself.

Ellen D., California Institution for Women, California
Possession
16 months

JUNE 30

TELLING MY STORY isn't easy because I have been in denial about my addiction for 25 years. But if nothing else, the treatment program at California Institute for Women has taught me to admit that.

It also taught me that I am most definitely powerless over my addiction. I know it's not my fault, but what I do about it is my responsibility.

Just like most of you who read this, I grew up in a very dysfunctional family. So I learned how to hide, stuff, and run from any bad feelings I may have had. Then as I grew older, I took comfort in a syringe, which led me to where I now sit.

This program has helped me to see that somewhere out there I have a Higher Power who thinks I am very special and that my feelings — whether they be bad or good — are okay.

Because of this program, for the first time in my life I like myself and feel like I'm somebody.

When I get released, I'm going into a recovery home so I don't lose my new outlook on life. It's a miracle in itself, because this program gave me back my hopes, my dreams, my life. With my dreams and the support I'll get upon my release, I feel I have a fighting chance to make it in the world.

Toni P., California Institution for Women, California
Possession for sale
16 months

I AM ONLY 26 years old. For 13 of them, I have been shooting and smoking dope as well as drinking.

In recovery, I have come to find out that I am powerless over my addiction to drugs and alcohol and the excitement I get from doing what it takes to feed my addiction.

It would be very easy to relapse, therefore it is essential that I get closer to my Higher Power as well as rely on peers who are in recovery, too.

I am also going to admit to my fear. I have my life in my own hands, but sometimes temptation is hard. That is why I find it necessary to give myself up completely to a group of others who are in recovery. Through them I can receive help when I have negative thoughts, but first I must desire it.

◆

Charles B., St. Clair Correctional Facility, Alabama
Murder, Burglary, Possession of narcotics
45 years

July 2

I ALWAYS THOUGHT I could change things when I was angry. In recovery, I've learned to do constructive things when I'm angry. When I get mad I walk away, think about it, and pray. If I would have followed those steps before, I wouldn't be in prison today.

I believe it takes a man to walk away from a fight, because anybody can fight or argue. When I was first told that, I said, "Man, that's jive." But after some serious thinking I understood what the phrase really means.

Running with the gangs isn't the answer. In the long run, behind a life like that you never know whose family is going to be in the front row at the funeral.

Love and take pride in yourself; if you don't, nobody will. It's your life, but please, think before it's too late.

I know if I can do it, you can, too. Put forth an effort to try to change a few things in society. I know sometimes it feels like there's no justice in the system, but if we keep striving for a better world, things can and will change.

◆

Carmece H., St. Clair Correctional Facility, Alabama
Murder, Attempted murder

I JOINED THE prison treatment program to try and find my personal inner feelings. I want to rediscover my feelings for myself as well as for my family and the people who really cared about me. But after so long of my foolish ways and not trying to better myself, I'm afraid they've given up hope.

I didn't make this decision to better myself on my own. I had a man "pull me up" and inspire me to give the program a chance. It's nerve-wracking and keeps me tensed up, but I'm trying to overcome that. The life I'm accustomed to isn't doing anything but keeping me in segregation and making it harder for me to get out in society. If and when I make it, I want to have a positive attitude out there and not come back into prison.

I want everything I've lost back. To me, the program is the first step. I have to earn and build up that trust again, and in general population, I couldn't do that. I spent years letting other priorities get in the way of my life, but no more.

◆

Steve L., St. Clair Correctional Facility, Alabama
Robbery, Theft of property, Breaking and entering
25 years

JULY 4

I FEEL LIKE recovery comes down to one thing: taking time out to take a close look at yourself. I used to keep myself distracted by life's distractions and never really slowed down to look at myself. Now I think before I speak and double-check my decisions before I act. That's what works for me.

◆

David V., St. Clair Correctional Facility, Alabama
Burglary, Forgery, Escape
23 years

I KNOW I need to be in this program because there's a lot I don't understand about my drug use. I know if I just stay in recovery and believe that God is with me, I'll do okay. God plays a big part in my life because without God, there's nothing I can do. I know God loves me because He brought me this way so I would wake up and see things for the way they are.

I have four kids who love me. They know I'm in prison, but they also know that I am in recovery, and they are glad that I am getting help. When I get out, I'm going to *stay* out. And this is how I truly feel.

◆

Andre F., St. Clair Correctional Facility, Alabama
Robbery

July 6

THIS HAS BEEN by far the hardest road that I have had to travel. Every day is a constant struggle to move forward to a better way of life. A lot of times I have to put my old addictive thinking into check. It's always there to tell me, "You don't have to go through all of this." "Wouldn't you much rather lay back and do nothing?" "You have things under control."

One thing it's right about is that for the most part, I have it under control because I call upon my Higher Power to give me the power I need to keep moving along. I tried to work a program for a long time without a Higher Power and found it to be like starting a car without any gas in it. My Higher Power gives me confidence, warmth, and a will to improve, day by day.

The main turning point for me was when I realized that I couldn't control my addiction, and I had to get gut-level honest with myself and others in order to get any kind of help. I knew I couldn't do it by myself; I needed some help. Through being open and honest with myself and those around me, I have found a greater understanding and awareness of myself that has proven to be very valuable.

It's all up to me. No matter how many programs or how many people try and help, it all lies within myself. All I have to do is reach in and get it.

◆

Steve F., St. Clair Correctional Facility, Alabama
Armed robbery
25 years

I HAVE SPENT my whole life searching for, but never finding out, who I really am.

Recovery has given me a chance to get in touch with my childhood, to explore and get in touch with the lost child, to feel and express the pain I suffered at the hands of my alcoholic parents.

As I begin to grow and mature mentally, I can feel pain and hurt without being afraid to show my emotions. I can forgive and love my parents. Recovery has taught me to be human, and as a human being, I will make mistakes. But I will no longer suffer for my parents' mistakes. I can now live my life, with all its successes and failures, one day at a time.

I feel I can forgive myself for my shortcomings because I have found and identified the lost child within me.

◆

Michael S., St. Clair Correctional Facility, Alabama
Armed robbery
25 years

JULY 8

SO FAR, MY personal experiences in recovery have been tremendously positive.

Before I came into the treatment program, I was a very negative and angry person. I realized I had those flaws. I admitted to myself that unless I changed, there was a very good possibility that I would spend the rest of my life in prison or quickly return if released. I also got in touch with and dealt with some very hurtful feelings that I had stuffed away inside of me, feelings I didn't even know I had.

Recovery is a hard road to travel, but unless I make up my mind to travel this road, I'd be on an inevitable path of self-destruction.

◆

Doug A., St. Clair Correctional Facility, Alabama
Murder
Life without parole

I NEVER REALIZED how my anger was pushing people away from me. My addiction drove my family away. Being in recovery helps me deal with my anger. Since I've been in recovery, I've been able to say I was wrong, when at one time in my life I couldn't admit it. Since I've been in recovery, I've been able to identify other problems, and I see that I have more problems in my life than I really knew. I can get help in recovery.

My spirituality means a lot to me. My Higher Power gives me all the strength and comfort I need to make it in recovery. When I first began my recovery I made a commitment to myself and my Higher Power that I was going to make a change in my life. I'm not going to tell anyone that recovery is easy, because it's not, but once you get into it, you'll begin to feel the changes in your life! I thank God for my treatment program. It has really helped me.

I'm a changed man. Recovery is the way.

◆

Lorenzo M., St. Clair Correctional Facility, Alabama
Murder
Life without parole

JULY 10

THERE ONCE WAS a time I hated myself, but since I've been in recovery, I have learned how to love myself and to love other people. There is so much I have learned in this program: how to forgive myself and other people and how to rebuild good relationships with people I had put out of my life.

When I came into the program, I had a lot of anger buried inside which had been hidden for a long time, but for the 18 months I've been in recovery, I have worked through a lot of it. I have looked at video tapes on anger, read books on anger, and went to seminars on it. I also talk about my feelings in my groups. By doing that, I now have peace of mind and can sleep better.

Another way I work on my anger is to write about it. Then at night before I go to bed, I take my notes and read them over and ask myself why I let myself get angry. If possible, I go and talk to those people and come to some understanding. That really helps.

◆

Edward M., St. Clair Correctional Facility, Alabama
Robbery
Life

THE PROGRAM HAS given me a lot of help with my problems. I didn't realize how much help I could get until I got here.

I am beginning to understand a lot of things about myself. I thought my life was over until I found the program. Right now I have a long way to go, but I know I can make it with the help of the people here.

◆

Carl S., St. Clair Correctional Facility, Alabama
Robbery
15 years

JULY 12

THERE HAS NEVER been a day I have not thought of my son. Never a reflection where I did not see his face. He is my heaven. I have caused him pain and misery, this I know, and to merely apologize and say "I am sorry" would never be enough. If I could be near him and hear him say "I love you" just one more time, the ugliness in me would be washed away and then I would be as close to goodness as I could ever be.

We all must have a goal and purpose in life. Mine is to see that my son, who I haven't seen since August of 1985, has a better life and more opportunity than I had, so he can give his children the love that I couldn't give him. And I want him to know that I love him more than life itself.

The way to do this is to get all the help I can for my disease of alcoholism. Because I believe if a person wants and desires something bad enough, he or she can achieve it.

◆

Danny T., St. Clair Correctional Facility, Alabama
Murder
Life

MY NATIONALITY IS Romanian. I have lived under the gypsy code all of my life. It was a code that few understood, where the foundation wasn't honesty, it was survival. Even though we lived under the same God who created the heavens and the earth, we always knew He understood our ways.

After 28 years of living under this code, I came to find myself in a great deal of trouble. Now, after five years of drug treatment and one year in St. Clair's program, I have found a new set of ethics and concepts that I apply to my life to get in touch with the true me. This new code has delivered me from alcohol and scheming and lying and manipulating, and helped me to get in touch with a Power greater than myself. I'm in a relationship with a true living God now who has granted me wisdom and salvation.

◆

Benjamin C., St. Clair Correctional Facility, Alabama
Robbery
12 years

JULY 14

IN 1983 I was released from Logan Correctional Center having finished a three-year sentence for forgery. That had been my fourth time to the joint. I had never been in treatment before, and the only Higher Power I knew was the "needle and cooker."

I had one thing going for me — a lovely wife and son who believed in me. My wife was a recovering addict. Together we made meetings and stayed clean. For the first time in my life I held down a job. I even went to a trade school. For nine years I stayed clean and sober.

Then tradegy struck. My wife was hit by a drunk driver and died. I was left alone to pick up the pieces. I believed I could do it alone. So I stopped going to meetings. I shunned the people who had been there for me for all those years. I turned back to the thing I thought I loved the most — drugs.

I was so bitter and hurt. I went on to lose my job, my house, and even my son. Then I forged two checks, and I had to go back to jail.

Now I'm back on the road of recovery. Although I'm in prison, there are A.A. and N.A. groups here. I'm not alone anymore. I'm not responsible for my disease, but I am responsible for my recovery. And my Higher Power, teaches me to keep coming back.

It works if you work it out sober, one day at a time.

Mike O., Logan Correctional Center, Illinois
Forgery
4 years

I WAS ADDICTED to cocaine, the number one killer. It controlled me for 19 years. It made my life so miserable, I wanted to commit suicide. I was a family man, but I lost my children and wife through my using. Nothing but heartache and pain. My addiction haunted me, day in and day out. It caused me to rob, steal, lie, and cheat. It made me lose my self-respect and took away my dignity and pride.

I had to admit that I was powerless.

Now that I am in recovery, I learned that I can maintain my life. I do it by sharing my feelings in my group and asking my Higher Power, who is God, to help me. I am doing better now. Through my recovery, I talk about things that are painful to me, and my group helps me to overcome them.

I am in prison for 10 years. But, fortunately, I am around other recovering addicts who love me. They have shown me I am unique and special.

The main thing I want to say is that recovery will work if we work it. We have to want it to work. Working the Twelve Steps is my recovery. So is staying around other recovering addicts like myself. Throughout my addiction, I never told anyone I loved them. But now I can say that I love you with all my heart and I care about you. Recovery will work for you, too. Good luck!

Nathaniel H., St. Clair Correctional Facility, Alabama
Distributing cocaine
10 years

JULY 16

I WAS BORN in San Juan, Puerto Rico. As a young man, I came to the United States to look for a better life. My English was pretty bad at the time; therefore, I couldn't find a good paying job. I thought that by selling drugs I would make the money I needed to support my family back in Puerto Pico.

It never occurred to me that I would get addicted to cocaine the very first time I used it. I did it thinking that all my problems would just go away. Instead I found myself with more serious problems.

I've been in prison three years and seven months. This time has helped me to understand and appreciate life better than ever. Even though I'm writing these few lines from a prison, I am now a happy man looking forward to a future.

◆

Benito R., St. Bride's Correctional Center, Virginia
Selling cocaine
19 years

I THOUGHT I could stop using drugs. I tried, then realized that I couldn't. I didn't understand why. Coming to this program, I understood that it wasn't my fault. It's a disease.

Now that I'm sober and getting an education, I can go back and see how I was hurting myself, my kids, and my parents. I thought that because I never let them see me after I got high or never was at home, I wasn't hurting them. But I was wrong. My kids needed me more than I thought. I can't say I was a good mother or daughter because I wasn't. Because of my addiction, I didn't see the pain they were going through.

It's time to take care of my disease and reach out and make up for all the pain I have caused myself and my family. I had never been to a drug program before — that's why I kept relapsing. But through this program I've learned how to build up my self-esteem, the warning signs to relapse, and the problems caused by the risks I took. I've been through a lot of emotional stress, but I try to accept my recovery no matter how painful it may be. We can all make it when we learn about ourselves and our disease. I can do it — and so can you. From one recovering addict to another, God bless us and give us the strength we need. We are not alone.

Sandra G., California Institution for Women, California
Petty theft with prior
16 months

JULY 18

I ALWAYS RAN from my problems before. When someone hurt me, I felt sorry for myself and ran from responsibility, not caring about anyone. I feel really bad about a lot of things I've done in my life.

Now I pray to my Higher Power to forgive my wrongdoings. My Higher Power means everything to me. I have awakened and realized that I want certain things in my life, and I know now — through experience — what to look for in others. I will never put myself or my family in this kind of pain again.

This program and my Higher Power have given me faith and more understanding about life. If I'm honest and love myself, then good things will come.

◆

John H., St. Clair Correctional Facility, Alabama
Robbery
25 years

TODAY IS ONE of those days when time seems so distant from reality. But my past hardships have given me the strength and knowledge to carry on in recovery by looking within myself where all my true problems lie.

At one time I fell prey to a mental and physical process in which I had no control — drug and alcohol addiction — and it caused me to make involuntary and absentminded decisions. It's said that money is the root of all evil. For me, it's drugs and alcohol. They are even more powerful than money, because money can be used for good measure, but drugs and alcohol will forever be a destructive force when in the hands of people out of control.

◆

Roland G., St. Clair Correctional Facility, Alabama
Theft, Escape
20 years

July 20

EVERYTHING THAT SURVIVES in life — both good and bad — starts with a strong foundation. Self-destruction is no different. It starts with bad childhood messages and low self-esteem, which is self-destruction's strong foundation. Next the walls go up. These walls are built with bricks of anger, hate, addiction, guilt, loneliness, and shame. To top it all off, the roof which keeps all this stuff together is denial.

To stop self-destruction, first we have to be sick and tired of being a failure, of prison, and of living the life we've been living. It all boils down to being sick and tired of being sick and tired. We must want a change. Once we've committed ourselves to change, we must start tearing down the house of self-destruction.

Digging up those past experiences can be rough, but through the pain we gain new strength. With this strength, we tear down the walls of our defects. We start to feel better about ourselves, and begin to disbelieve those childhood messages. We dig up that old foundation of low self-esteem and a new foundation is laid — one built of commitment, pride, and self-respect. We construct new walls of love, trust, forgiveness, acceptances, confidence, and courage. The roof of this new house is our recovery program. This house remains strong as long as we keep the roof on it.

◆

Billy S., St. Clair Correctional Facility, Alabama
Robbery
21 years

I'M DOING TIME for burglary, and being a repeat offender, the court sentenced me to life in prison even though my crimes were non-violent. My life has been up and down, I didn't know how to make the right decisions or manage my life. Now that I've entered the program, I've learned about all my hidden anger. I've learned how to express and share my problems so that I can get some input that might help me.

Life goals are very important to me. In program, I learned about setting immediate, intermediate, and ultimate goals in life. My goals are very proper because I know where I'm at. I know why I'm here in prison — and I know where I want to go. To set goals, I have to write them down, outline my plans, and determine the rewards and benefits from realizing them. I visualize myself reaching my goals and think of them daily.

My goals are to be sober and become successful. My ultimate goal is to help younger people who are not aware of the seriousness of stress, hidden anger, addictions, loneliness, abuse, and sexual issues. Love and recovery are what's encountered in the St. Clair's treatment program. I want to share what I've learned with people in everyday life, who aren't aware of how this program works.

◆

Jimmy D., St. Clair Correctional Facility, Alabama
Robbery
Life

I AM CURRENTLY on a life without parole (LWOP) sentence for capital murder. The circumstances surrounding my case are very unusual. Due to pending legal proceedings, I won't go into that.

Here's the deal. For a long time I struggled with a lot of guilt for being even remotely involved. A lot of this guilt came from the pain and embarrassment the case brought my family. I wasn't entirely self-destructive, but I seriously disliked myself.

I was able to overcome this, in part, because of my involvement in treatment, but also from a spiritual retreat. I made a list of the things that bothered me and a list of the good aspects of my life. A fire was lit in a bucket, and all of us threw our bad lists in the fire, and held our good lists in our hands and prayed for forgiveness. A tremendous weight was lifted from me. I was able to regain my self-respect and to stop hating myself and the others involved. I feel now that the pain I experienced is giving way to a new and improved me.

◆

Greg B., St. Clair Correctional Facility, Alabama
Murder
Life without parole

MY STORY IS about relapse. I've been in trouble with drugs for almost 16 years now. I started using drugs when I was nine years old. I was smoking reefer with my mother and step-dad. Drugs became a habit at an early age for me.

My drug use caused me all kinds of trouble, like social problems with friends and family. As I got older, I couldn't keep up in school. The drug use stunted my emotional growth and my learning ability so that I thought and acted like a person about three to five years younger than myself. In the 10th grade, I quit school to work with my dad to help support my drug habit. I started to use stronger drugs, but through all of this I knew one day I would have to stop. I tried to quit for periods of times, like say three months, but I never made it. This went on for about seven or eight years.

Now I'm in prison and for the first time I am getting my life together. I feel good about myself. I no longer need drugs. I am in a treatment program here. I've gotten more help and come farther in 45 days than in all the years I tried to quit by myself.

◆

Rayford R., St. Clair Correctional Facility, Alabama
Attempted murder
20 years

JULY 24

THERE IS A belief that there is no way out of drug addiction. But in my opinion, there is a way out of using drugs. It takes a Higher Power as we know Him. And, if we were to realize ourselves as a source of hope, we can attain heights greater than what we are accustomed to believe are possible.

Addiction doesn't end quickly. Sometimes it is a gradual decrease in one's consumption of drugs, especially crack or cocaine.

The key is faith in Narcotics Anonymous. Other addicts are another source. My message is that there is hope.

◆

August C., Louisiana State Penitentiary, Louisiana
Armed robbery
20 years

COCAINE AND HEROIN were my first loves. I still remember the day drugs came into my life. They made me feel so good, so special — like a man. Right away I knew they were for me.

I was having such a good time, I completely forgot all of my problems and my family who loved me. But my addiction kept telling me everything would be all right, not to worry. And I listened. Even those times I went to jail over and over, even then I knew drugs would be waiting for me as always. But after awhile, they turned on me. I couldn't get rid of them. They made me hate myself — and still I wanted them.

Now I have found new hope — a Higher Power, much greater than drugs and myself. Now I thank my Higher Power every day, and we talk and He understands me. Through Narcotics Anonymous I am learning to deal with myself and understand my obsession with drugs. My Higher Power has taken over my life now. It feels real good to be clean and sober. And I'll have N.A. upon my release.

I still have problems and some difficult times, but with my Higher Power and N.A., I can deal with them clean and sober. I have new friends just like me, and they care. Drugs may want me back, but I don't want them.

Michael A., Logan Correctional Facility, Illinois
Burglary
4 years

JULY 26

SOME TIME AGO I was imprisoned in a dungeon of dark depression. I was relentlessly tormented by confused, anxious thoughts. My back was painfully bowed from the heavy burdens of guilt and bitterness I carried with me constantly. I despised living this way, but I was bound so tightly by chains of hopelessness that escape seemed impossible. Every day seemed like the one before it, and soon I lost all interest in life.

In desperation, I called on a friend to help me, a friend who had never let me down. I poured out all my problems to God, and in faith, I placed each care into God's loving hands. My tensions eased, and I felt a wonderful, unexplainable peace. I admitted the wrongdoings that had haunted me for so long. Then I had to forgive those who had harmed me.

I was so happy with these victories, and soon the sweet fragrance of thankfulness swallowed up the foul atmosphere of self-pity. At that moment I realized the prison doors of my dark dungeon had swung wide open. Rejoicing, I walked out into the fresh, clean air of God's freedom. Sometimes, if I am not careful, I am tempted to once again visit the dungeon. But I think about the terribleness of that place, and, with the help of my Friend, I flee from it speedily!

◆

Harold C., Nottoway Correctional Center, Virginia
Rape, Sodomy
2 life sentences plus 6 years

I'M GETTING TO know myself over again, getting to know the real me.

I was born to two loving and non-drinking people. I was an only child and sometimes it was lonely, even though I had a lot of young cousins to play with. I began to run with the big boys. They drank, so I did, too. I was 17 years old. I could drink more than the men I ran with, and it was almost as if I couldn't get drunk.

In 1968 I quit school and went into the army where I drank to overcome my fear of not living to come home again. After I got out of the army, my father and I had a disagreement, and I left home. I drank, but went back to school, got a G.E.D., and trained to be an over-the-road tractor-trailer driver.

During all this time I never thought that I would see my dad alive again. I was right. Dad died, and then my son died two years later. I drank the pain away.

I came to prison in 1980, was out in '81, drank all the more. I did okay until 1985. I'm back in prison, but this time I found something — or should I say it found me. It's called recovery. I'm glad either way because I have a new and joyful life, thanks to recovery. If you want what I have, admit you're powerless over your addiction, and come to believe in a Power greater than yourself.

◆

Paul P., Ventress Correctional Facility, Alabama
17 years

JULY 28

AS AN ADDICT I thought I was in total control of my life. I had to control every situation. Little did I know at the time that I was actually out of control. In my confused state of mind I really believed what I was doing was okay, and no one could have told me I was wrong.

Now I have come to the realization that I was wrong. I was completely powerless over my behavior. Now that I can think straight again, I can see where I'm wrong.

I have come to believe that I can't make it on my own. I have to let my Higher Power take control of my life, and lead me on the right path of life. I am powerless over my life and need to turn the power over to my Higher Power. This is the only way I can continue to live and grow. It is absolutely necessary that I turn my will over. This is the only way for me to attain true inner peace.

◆

Sam B., Ventress Correctional Facility, Alabama
Murder

I HAVE BEEN in and out of prison for years. I have always been a self-centered person. All my life people have been doing things for me; not only did I expect it, but I was ungrateful and I resented them because they didn't do more. I wondered why I should help others, when I believed they were supposed to be helping me. I thought that if others had trouble, they deserved it. I was full of anger, self-pity, and resentment.

Somewhere along the way, I learned that helping others without thought of getting something for it could overcome my obsession with being selfish. I understood for the first time in my life what humility was all about. Today I know what it's like to have peace and serenity in my life. Even behind bars, locked up 24 hours a day, I have peace and serenity in my heart. And I don't have to use drugs or alcohol to feel good.

◆

Jerry E., St. Clair Correctional Facility, Alabama
Robbery III
20 years

JULY 30

JUST WHAT IS "hope" to an alcoholic? Is it a name? Is it just a word that a person doesn't know anything about?

Hope to me as a recovering alcoholic is much more than that. Because, you see, before this broken-up body was cast into chemical bondage, I was a father just like millions of other fathers who live in this great nation of ours. Hope to me was something that was created many years ago. And it's a God-sent inspiration for me each and every day I wake up.

I give thanks to God that He blessed me with the hope that helped me overcome my many problems. For you see, Hope is the name of my daughter. I've never seen her. I've never talked to her. I've never held her tightly in my arms. But she is the source of all of my strength. And it is God's love sent through her that has helped me overcome my chemical problems and find the true meaning of the word "hope."

◆

Rothen H., Louisiana State Penitentiary, Louisiana
Aggravated sexual battery
Life

A LOT OF people may think that because someone is locked up, the alcohol problem is no longer there. Not true!

In prisons throughout the world, it is a sad fact that alcohol is readily available for those who seek it. It is very hard to resist, and it makes me angry that, at times, I am unable to resist. I feel completely powerless over alcohol, and it is very depressing and gives me low self-esteem.

However, even though I go through those difficult times, I am able to control my urge because of the Higher Power that is mentioned in the Twelve Steps. That is what makes me strong. On the streets I knew of a Higher Power, but not until I was locked up and given the chance to meditate and think was I able to fully understand Him.

A.A. has given me my sanity back and helped me to realize that I do not need alcohol in my life. So to all of you out there with a problem, be strong, stick with A.A., and when and if you find that Higher Power, *don't let go!* He is real, and there is a solution.

◆

Greg B., Louisiana State Penitentiary, Louisiana
Aggravated sexual battery
13 years

AUGUST 1

AS AN INMATE, it's hard to live with the negativity within the prison environment. I had to blot out the thought of giving up. Seeing only a few who wanted to change, it was a challenge to me to want to recover. My friends said, "What's the use of giving up drugs now, while in prison? Life is over." However, I felt that the recovery role models in my program gave me the boost I needed to stay strong in my struggle for sobriety.

It was a special challenge to admit I had a drug problem. I was so ashamed of my past behavior. Most addicts who live a degrading and useless life don't have any concern for anyone but themselves. We tend to feel that we can handle drugs, only to find out later while sitting in a jail cell how big a fool King Heroin had made of us.

But, after I made a decision to turn my life over to my Higher Power, I was able to rely on Him and not myself. Then I was able to try and make amends to my wife whom I had hurt. She then saw the sincerity of a changed man.

I learned and applied the Twelve Steps to my daily life in prison, which wasn't easy. But it's the real challenge that makes us strong enough to face our problems. I want to be an example of a man who came into prison an addict and left a sober and sane human being.

Harold R., Louisiana State Penitentiary, Louisiana
Possession with intent to distribute
15 years

STEP ELEVEN: SOUGHT through prayer and meditation to improve our conscious contact with God *as we understood Him*, praying only for knowledge of His will for us and the power to carry that out.

I am conscious of someone greater than myself watching every move I make. That alone keeps me thinking of God, and I am reluctant to do things that weaken the mind and spirit. Step Eleven has given me a spiritual awakening, and the peace of mind and courage to change the things I can in my life.

I thank my God for keeping me strong. I challenge all addicts to begin treatment toward recovery. Maybe, just maybe, we can make a real difference in our children's lives. I pray to get the chance to go free and give back what A.A., N.A., and my Higher Power have given to me — a new lease on life.

◆

Harold R., Louisiana State Penitentiary, Louisiana
Possession with intent to distribute
15 years

August 3

LET ME SAY right now that I have no education, so it's hard for me to put this into words.

I have 35 years for armed robbery. All my life I have been a drunk and a dope head, dependent on my family. When I came to prison, I went through all kinds of withdrawals. I got write-up after write-up, and nobody could tell me anything.

If I hadn't gotten such a long sentence, I would be dead. I thank God and all the great social workers who have convinced me to get back on the right road. With a lot of hard work, anyone can change their life if they want to. I believe I have. With God's help, I am going to make something of my life from here on out.

◆

Jerry H., Louisiana State Penitentiary, Louisiana
Armed robbery
35 years

I SPENT NINE years in a Texas prison, and in that nine years I didn't have a drop to drink. When I got released I started drinking again. I was out less than four months before I received 30 more years here in Alabama.

It just goes to show that abstinence is not sobriety.

At that time, Texas didn't have a program like the one I found here. I'm learning a lot about myself and my problems, and I hope that whenever I'm released, I can be the son, father, brother, friend, and citizen that I should have always been.

I'm having to deal with a lot of emotions in this program, but that is what it's set up to do — to bring all those hidden emotions up from where we hid them by submerging them in alcohol and drugs. But this time when those emotions come up, I can deal with them sober and with a lot of friends in my support group.

This program is the best thing that has happened to me in years. The first line of our philosophy goes like this — "We have awakened and realized that where we are in our lives is not where we want to be." It feels good to be awake and thinking more clearly than I have in years. Wake up, brothers and sisters, and live.

◆

Frank F., St. Clair Correctional Facility, Alabama
Attempted rape
30 years

August 5

I HAVE ONLY been in the drug program for a total of nine days and have not had much time to really get into it. Nonetheless, I have had some interesting experiences in regard to the house rules and the individual attitudes of various family members.

I was transferred to my current correctional facility due to a disturbance that took place at another correctional facility. Because of the tense environment that I was forced to live in for approximately 18 months, I still experience difficulties dealing with seemingly bad attitudes from individuals. When I first began in the program, I met with various personalities that seemed, for all practical purposes, to be of an unfriendly nature.

At first, these experiences caused negativity within me and almost caused me to change my mind about attending the program. I found myself allowing anger to cloud my thinking and this began to reflect through my actions. If not for the love and concern of several residents, I would probably have requested to be removed from the program without having given it a fair trial. Fortunately, I received the help that I needed from some concerned family members who helped me overcome my anger and negativity. Now I feel I have conquered an important step and can continue working to better myself.

◆

Roger J., St. Clair Correctional Facility, Alabama
Burglary
50 years

I HAVE BECOME involved with the prison's treatment program to work on my problems. I thought that I only had two problems — drugs and anger. But I've been shown that my life has had more problems than I realized. I have committed to change my life and become a more effective person both now and whenever I get out.

I have been to prison three times since 1984, but I always did the wrong things out there in the free world and had to come back. I never committed myself seriously to any program in prison, but now I have awakened and realized that I have to change my habits or stay in prison the rest of my life.

The program offers steps to help me change, and I am going to take advantage of them. My anger problem is bad and I stuff my feelings a lot, but I am learning self-control on my temper and how to deal with my feellngs. I thank God and the people who are interested in my changing and living right. I am going to change this time, no doubt, with help.

My Higher Power directed me to treatment so I can learn my problems and get my life straightened out once and for all. My Higher Power will continue to lead me the right way.

◆

Jeff H., St. Clair Correctional Facility, Alabama
Burglary, Possession of marijuana
57 years

August 7

I FOUND FREEDOM through recovery in a maximum-security prison by submitting to God. I was released from my addiction, which was more powerful than the crimes I had committed. It was released when I took the First Step in the recovery program and admitted complete defeat, believing that God could and would relieve me of my addiction if He were asked.

The day I took Step One I could feel the presence of God as I jumped down off my bunk, got down on my knees, and asked God to forgive me. Somewhere deep down inside, I knew that I would have to confess my wrongdoing to some other person, just as it's suggested in the recovery program that had given me my freedom back.

I pray for the freedom and peace which passes all understanding. I pray for that freedom and peace which the world can neither give nor take away.

◆

Tom S., St. Clair Correctional Facility, Alabama
Kidnapping
23 years

I'M WRITING TO you about self-love. I have a problem with this because I grew up beating myself up for events that I had no control over. Yet I would always say, "I could have done something!"

I've been here in recovery for almost two months. After my mom passed away back in '88, I hated myself and everyone around me. I believed I could have saved my mother's life. She passed away after a massive heart attack. Even though they said there was nothing I could do, I believed there was.

I'm starting to learn that in order for me to build relationships, I must go through a grieving process for my mother. I can't build relationships with others unless I'm able to be at peace and love myself. If I'm constantly beating myself up and hating myself, sooner or later, I'm going to take that anger out on someone else.

Now I'm learning to love myself and accept that there are some things that I have no control over. And it's good to have people I can trust to talk to and get my anger out.

◆

James F., St. Clair Correctional Facility, Alabama
Assault

I HAVE GAINED periods of six months and up to one-and-a-half years of sobriety only to relapse. The reason I relapsed is because I slacked off and quit doing the things necessary for me to maintain — not going to enough meetings, going around old playmates and playgrounds, and all the rest.

The last time I relapsed was worse than any other time. The price always gets higher. I had a car wreck and killed my wife while driving under the influence of alcohol.

It has taken working the program for me to come to grips with what happened and to learn to forgive myself and to try to go on with my life. At one point I was spiritually bankrupt. I used the group as my Higher Power, but eventually I started getting some of my spirituality back. I would thank God for keeping me clean every night before I went to sleep, and that would be the first thought on my mind when I woke up the next morning. I would pray and ask His help and protection to stay clean for that day. When I quit doing this or don't do it as often — I mean like every day — that's when I get close to a relapse.

◆

Rickey H., St. Clair Correctional Facility, Alabama
Criminal negligent homicide
27 years

ONE MINUTE OF your life, one act of uncontrolled anger, can cost you greatly, to the point of spending the rest of your life in prison. It can also cause you to be condemned to death. Not learning how to deal with anger usually will result in a life full of pain, broken relationships, loneliness, shame, guilt, despair, and overwhelming helplessness.

How do I know this? Because I've been there. I turned to drugs and alcohol for some temporary release from the pain, and each time that fix was gone, the pain was stronger and the anger deeper. And, in one moment of anger and irrational behavior, I killed someone. I live with that every day. I live with the pain and grief I have caused that man's family, my own family, and myself. And it was so senseless and avoidable.

Anger is a natural emotion, just like love or fear. There is nothing wrong with feeling anger, but we must learn how to deal with it. We must learn where it comes from and why. Most anger is misguided, it is directed at someone who really has nothing to do with the depth of the anger.

We all must stop and take a hard look at ourselves and our lives. Life is precious and meant to be enjoyed. And time keeps ticking away.

◆

John D., St. Clair Correctional Facility, Alabama
Manslaughter
30 years

August 11

In prison, I first began to reexperience my spirituality in a group of recovering addicts and alcoholics where people talked about true and difficult things, things that are so painful, that it touched the hole in their soul. At that point in time, I felt a certain warmth and a feeling of healing that touched the hole in my own soul. When healing takes place, the walls, floors, and ceiling become sacred, and the room becomes a holy place. At those moments I don't feel like I'm in prison. I feel a sense of warmth and love. I know during this time that my Higher Power is there with me.

◆

DeWitt C., St. Clair Correctional Facility, Alabama
Possession of narcotics
18 years

I BELIEVE THAT the whole key to my recovery was admitting my extremely low self-esteem. The majority of my issues have stemmed from that. My stealing, drugging, and sexual issues were all cover-ups for it. My low self-esteem was a deep-rooted problem that I refused to recognize for years.

When I stole, I did it to possess "things," to make me acceptable to others. When I stole hot-rods and bikes, I did so to gain recognition. When I was high or drunk, I put on a false bravado which helped me impress those around me.

My sexual issues — verbal and physical abuse of women and rape — were a search for a feeling of power I wanted to control another person to feel in command.

Once I admitted that I was powerless over my life and honestly admitted the source of my deviant behaviors, only then could I begin a sincere recovery program. After 16 months of intense treatment, I have only just scratched the surface. This road will be long and hard.

◆

Dale F., St. Clair Correctional Facility, Alabama
Rape
Life

AUGUST 13

MY GOALS ARE to get out of prison and support my wife and children. I have two boys.

I've learned a lot about childhood messages from being in this program, and I realize that a lot of the problems I've had in life came from my childhood. I had never given it any thought until coming into this program. I'm thankful, because I'm understanding myself and the reasons for my being where I am in my life.

I spend a lot of time thinking of what's going on in my kids' lives. I don't want them growing up and doing the things I have and ending up in prison.

I thank God for my children. I know in my heart that He will look over them and keep them in good health. My faith will always be with me. Without God in my life, I wouldn't be here today receiving help for the problems I have.

◆

Ricky H., St. Clair Correctional Facility, Alabama
Escape
30 years

THE FIRST TIME I was in the program, I felt in my heart that I wanted it, but I had so much negative stuff inside of me that I let that win over recovery.

I focused entirely on what other people did to me. When people pulled me up on my negative behavior, I felt they were trying to hurt me instead of help me. Every time somebody brought something negative that I was doing to my attention, I would justify it by saying that the person disliked me because I was black. Having this kind of attitude got me terminated from the program.

I went back out into population and took a good look around me. The main thing that slapped me in the face was that in order to survive in population, I had to live the same kind of lifestyle that I'd lived on the street. This was the only way I knew because I didn't apply myself to learning anything else.

So I came back to the program and took a good look at what was being brought to my attention by other people. I realized this stuff hurt me because it was the truth. This time I've applied the concepts of the program to my life, and I slowly began to realize that whites weren't doing anything to me because I was black. They told me the truth because they loved and cared about me. And I learned to love them for caring.

◆

Herman L., St. Clair Correctional Facility, Alabama
Possession and sale of cocaine
20 years

August 15

I'M 35 YEARS old and in prison for the fifth time. At about the age of 10 I got high for the first time. Talk about cool, man, I was the coolest dude there was. By the time I was 12 I was into the big stuff — huffing Right Guard, lighter fluid, glue, and gas.

I progressed to LSD and then started trying to turn my friends on. Some took, some refused. When I was 24, I was in prison for the third time. I knew that if I did not change, I'd be in deep trouble the rest of my life. I swore I was through with drugs. I got out, and in less than three months, I was back in jail.

I always was proud of myself for never using a needle to get high. I'd done drugs for 19 years before I gave in and tried one. Before the month was out I was using the needle 20 to 30 times a night and stealing anything that I could trade for a shot.

The last time I saw my grandmother was when I took $140 from her to buy more coke. Now she is dead. That lady raised me since I was six years old, and I treated her like dirt, just to get high and be cool.

So now I'll have to get it together. No one can do this but me. I alone will have to make up my mind and decide. But thanks to A.A. and N.A., I can get support from people who can relate to me and help me stay away from drugs. And you know what? *That's cool.*

◆

Lester T., Louisiana State Penitentiary, Louisiana
Aggravated burglary
15 years

I'M LIKE MOST rerounders. I entered a drug treatment program as a bargain with my relatives to save our family. I just went through the motions in treatment. I wasn't there for myself, I was there for my relatives. I felt the Twelve Step program was a bunch of statistical nonsense. I felt my willpower was stronger than anything the program was offering. "I can quit any time I want," I used to say.

After my stay was up, I was ready to show my folks and friends I had conquered my addiction without participating in the program. I had done it on my own. Forty-eight hours later I had relapsed. This particular relapse was 10 times worse than before I entered the program.

So from this recovering addict: Yes, I needed a Higher Power. Yes, I needed a Twelve Step Program, and yes, I needed a sponsor before I reached the point of no return resulting in death or lifetime confinement.

◆

Kelvin A., Ventress Correctional Facility, Alabama
Theft of property
15 years

AUGUST 17

THIS THING WE call "pride" can get us into a lot of trouble — from disciplinaries to never getting out of prison, even to coming back to prison once we are released.

After many years of having to "defend" my pride, and after a particular incident where I almost lost all chance of ever getting out of prison, I had to slam on the brakes and ask myself, "What is going on here?" I discovered that I, as a recovering inmate, have to determine which is most important — my freedom or my pride? If it's my pride, then my chances of getting out of prison and staying out are very slim. But if my freedom is of the utmost importance, then I have already taken a very large step toward recovery.

The freedom that I am speaking of is not just physical freedom, but also the spiritual and psychological freedom from chemical bondage.

I had to decide which one would take priority in my life — freedom or pride? I couldn't have both.

◆

James G., Ventress Correctional Facility, Alabama
Murder
Life

As a CONVICTED felon, I always wanted to be tough even though I was easygoing on the inside. I did things to appear tough for so long that I became a person you did not cross. Word was, I didn't bother anyone, but I didn't take no mess.

I came from a family where alcohol was always available. All the trouble I've ever gotten into has been because of drinking. But I never associated my troubles or my problems with my addiction. Then one night I was drinking alone in a bar when some friends dropped in and invited me to go out with them for some fun. Drunk, my friends and I robbed seven people on different stops. By morning, I'd had at least two blackouts. But I remembered one of my friends had killed a man in cold blood.

Now that I'm in prison, there's no denying the trouble alcohol has caused me. But I am in A.A. and treatment. Now I'm free from the inside out, and I have a new love, respect, and trust for myself. Although I'm still locked up, I do not want to use. My body, mind, and heart are clean and sober. I have not regretted any part of my recovery. I look forward to things like group meetings and A.A. Now I'm not just a convicted felon, I'm part of a recovery program that works.

◆

Billy T., Ventress Correctional Facility, Alabama
Murder
Life

MY STORY DOESN'T differ from any other addict who has abused drugs for 25 years. There was no excuse too small or too large that wasn't a good excuse to use.

I'm 43 years old, and my arrest and conviction record is very long. It started at the age of 16 in the Illinois Youth Commission, moving on to Cook County Jail, Pontiac, Stateville, and in the country of Mexico. I graduated through a painful system. I continued to use drugs. Each conviction was for drugs. Even this current period of incarceration is for possession of a controlled substance.

I believe motivation can come from a combination of desperation and inspiration. It was desperation that ran me to an N.A. meeting here at Logan Correctional Center and inspiration that kept me coming back. After reading the N.A. literature and working the Twelve Steps, my attitude, thinking, and values began to change. I began to regain my dignity, self-love, self-esteem, self-worth, and self-respect.

By studying the N.A. literature and working the Twelve Steps for the 30 months of incarceration, I'm not just on the program, I'm in recovery. I'm not just clean and sober; I have a total lifestyle change. That's recovery!

◆

Eddie S., Logan Correctional Center, Illinois
Sale of a controlled substance
8 years

I KNOW WHAT God has done for me in my life. I'm not the same man I used to be. My thinking has made a 180-degree turn. I don't have the same desires that I used to have. I don't talk or act like I used to. I enjoy life now. Life is worth living when you have God to go through life with. I have peace in my heart now, and that is something I don't ever remember having when I was on the streets.

There are a lot of hurting people in the free world. And in prison. I'm not saying it's easy, but I know that God can lift my burdens. God can do for me what I could not do for myself. I wish everyone could have peace in their hearts. I can't give it to them, but I know who can — God.

As I said, I don't ever remember having peace when I was on the streets. Now I do.

◆

Jerry M., St. Clair Correctional Facility, Alabama
Rape, Sodomy
95 years

AUGUST 21

MORE THAN A decade may go by before I'm allowed to live in the free world again. I'm trying to realistically prepare for the adjustment.

I possess a crucial element, I think: I now believe I'm worth it. Not only am I worth the potential pleasures life has to offer — the material things and being admired and respected — but I'm also worth the struggles that are certain to come. The man who I am now is willing to deal with the hardships in an effort to remain the changing person I am.

No, I'm not perfect, but I feel decent. Perhaps *that* is perfection. I am *now* willing to change and grow, to stumble in some endeavors but continue to take on others. I'm only human, right?

It's ironic, the more I change nowadays, the more I want to keep changing. I'm a better man now, a better person, than I have ever been. It would be foolish not to improve upon this, no matter what happens.

◆

Michael M., Graham Correctional Center, Illinois
Attempted murder, Multiple robberies

BEFORE I WAS arrested, my life was controlled by drugs. I was trapped by my need for the instant gratification that drugs gave me. For a long time it was pleasurable. Then I saw the ugly side of addiction. The higher drugs took me, the lower they brought me.

After I was arrested, I looked for another way of life. I decided to turn my will and life over to the care of my Higher Power. This is the Third Step in Narcotics Anonymous, but it was my first step in recovery from drug addiction. I made the decision — it was not made for me.

I also came to realize that spiritual growth through my Higher Power is the force that helps me to change and become more tolerant, patient, and useful to others in their recovery from drug addiction.

◆

Samuel M., Western Missouri Correctional Center, Missouri
Intent to distribute marijuana
10 years

WHEN I WAS presented with the opportunity to participate in this book, I was very eager to express myself in the most important aspect of my life — recovery.

The only successful method I know for maintaining sobriety is through treatment, awareness, and education. I have come to the conclusion that getting addicted to drugs is a process, making it all the more certain that recovery is also a process.

I say this because of personal experience and from my observations of other inmates. I used to say I could not do my 10-year sentence sober. I often hear others say they need drugs to make it through. But the most often-used excuse is that something has gone wrong at home. I used this excuse myself. But the question became, how could something that had caused so much harm help me and my family work out our problems?

I have come to realize that I'm a much better person off drugs. I have my Higher Power, who has endowed me with the power to do anything within reason without drugs. Although I'm not a professional by academic achievements, I am an expert from years of experience as a user. I am an inmate and a rerounder. I used to think I had the strength to use again. But now I know I have the strength not to use drugs. That is my personal experience today.

◆

Kerry B., Western Missouri Correctional Center, Missouri
Sale of cocaine
10 years

TODAY, OR MAYBE it was yesterday or the day before, we doubted our value to society, to our family and friends, and to ourselves. Often we travel from day to day with no direction. That is normal given the human condition and the effects of incarceration.

The length of time we spend traveling on this "lost highway," uncertain of ourselves, is equal to the time it takes us to find the *true* guide within us. We all have this reality of truth within us, and we can determine which is the right and which is the wrong direction extending from the crossroads under our feet. We do have a choice. No matter if we are limited by four walls of a prison cell, living at home with our family, or standing on a mountain peak where the boundaries are further than the eyes can see, we are faced with the choice.

Searching within ourselves may be unfamiliar and not an easy reaction for many of us, but we can learn to respond in this way with practice once we decide to grow toward this true direction. When we open ourselves to this positive urging and are willing to follow it, we will unfold and discover a beautiful side of ourselves.

If we take some time each day and quiet our thoughts long enough to sense our true direction, we can be certain that it's right for us. All we need to do is make a decision to listen.

◆

Daniel S., Western Missouri Correctional Center, Missouri
Possession and sale of heroin
7 years

AUGUST 25

RECOVERY FROM DRUG and alcohol addiction is a long, hard road. Most people in jail are there as a result of crimes committed to obtain drugs.

To recover, we addicts must progress from the denial stage and admit there is a problem with drugs or alcohol before we can accept that addiction continues to bring us back to jail. We must be honest enough to confront the fears that lead us to escape life on life's terms.

Acceptance is next. We need to accept deep down where the fear and the pain comes from, and accept that we have scared and hurt people by our actions.

Then we must be willing to allow someone else to help us. We need to diligently ask for help, and take the suggestions offered us in the Twelve Step program and by other recovering people.

If we change nothing, nothing changes within us. If we fail and are lucky, we might come back to jail. But a lot of us die.

◆

Vicky R., Dwight Correctional Facility, Illinois
Armed robbery
6 years

I WAS IN the hospital, shackled to my bed reading a religious newspaper, when I came across the prayer by St. Francis of Assisi. I cut it out of the paper and sent it home to Mom. I got out of jail, got rearrested, and wound up back in prison. A little voice in the back of my head kept telling me I needed help. I decided to go and get it because I knew it wasn't going to come to me. That's when I first got into the program.

I was attending Cocaine Anonymous and Narcotics Anonymous meetings when I came across the St. Francis prayer again, as it was recited at the end of meetings. Upon coming to a meeting, I opened a book of A.A. stories and there it was again — "Lord, make me an instrument of your peace."

My Higher Power works in mysterious ways, and I believe He's trying to tell me something through that prayer. I now have a better outlook on aspects of my life. With faith, determination, and help from my Higher Power, I can beat this thing that's been beating me most of my life. The way I look at it, when you've got nothing, you've got nothing to lose!

◆

Deborah T., Dwight Correctional Facility, Illinois
Burglary
3 years

AUGUST 27

IN RECOVERY I find that it isn't drugs that I'm fighting, it's my feelings and the way I see things. Through my stay in treatment, I've found peace by seeing others like me who have had an addictive life. We don't talk so much about drugs as about needing a new attitude. We work on maintaining a positive thought pattern, and we help bring up each other's awareness.

I find that a spiritual belief is the best addition to life. We also help build our self-esteem. We learn to believe in ourselves and others. All this comes from being honest with each other.

I try to learn all I can. This is the only way to help myself. By thinking back to my childhood days, I bring up past events that caused me bad feelings. Then I receive input from others. We relate with each other all the time. Ideas like honesty, commitment, confidence, trust, forgiveness, love, consistency, and more we try to instill in everyday life. We take things seriously. We motivate each other. We see each other as a family.

◆

Henry T., St. Clair Correctional Facility, Alabama
Attempted murder
25 years

EARLY IN TREATMENT, when I heard the problems and personal experiences of others, I got so overcome with emotions that it actually felt like the problems of others were really problems that I didn't know I had. Or I would try to sweep my problems under a rug and think they went away, when actually I was trying to ignore them.

I have come to the conclusion that self-help is a wonderful thing for me, and group help is even more so. I have had good and bad experiences in life. But I am on the road to recovery by admitting that I have a problem in the first place. I have to love myself to want to help myself; at times helping others comes easier.

I denied that I had a problem before I came to treatment, but since I've seen and heard the problems of others, my problems have come to the surface and I'm starting to deal with them one day at a time.

With the help of other recovering addicts and the help of God, I can apply my own self-help and recover.

◆

John M., St. Clair Correctional Facility, Alabama
Burglary
Life without parole

AT A YOUNG age, I fell in love with the streets. My life slowly slipped away into trouble, and as a result of my criminal behavior, prison is where I landed.

I got out of prison in 1980, but I still had a criminal mind, attitude, and behavior. I started forging checks. I did this to support my cocaine and heroin addiction. I also embezzled $25,000 from a bank. I went to prison as a result, which is where I am today.

I am now working a program using the Twelve Steps and Twelve Traditions in A.A. and N.A. My recovery is very important to me. I have accepted that I am powerless over drugs and alcohol. I also have experienced feelings of loneliness and the fear of getting out of prison.

I have had a spiritual awakening. God is a very important part of my life today and of my recovery. I realize if it were not for God, I would not have a second chance. Now I feel that I can return to society and live a productive life, sober and happy about myself.

Since being incarcerated, I have gained an Associate Degree in Arts from Faulkner University in hopes that I can get a good job when I get out of prison.

May God bless all the inmates who read this book.

◆

Harvey R., Bullock Correctional Facility, Alabama
Forgery, Embezzlement
9 years

THERE ARE THREE things that all of us, especially prisoners, want and need most: peace of mind, hope for the future, and freedom. Not the kind of freedom the parole board can give, but freedom from the fear, loneliness, and sense of hopelessness that most prisoners live with much of the time.

It took some time for me to admit responsibility for my crime. Then when I looked back on what I did wrong, everything blew up in my face. But as I go to some of the meetings around here, we talk about how to use our time and other things about life. If we're to beat the odds, we need to know how to use the time inside prison to our advantage.

If we can use the time inside to break habits that got us in trouble, then those months or years need not be wasted. It is quite possible for a determined prisoner to obtain a high school diploma, get some vocational training, or even a college degree. Certainly, we can get help in kicking substance abuse.

◆

Nathaniel G., Easterling Corrections Facility, Alabama
18 months

BENEATH ALL OF the reasoning we could offer as to why we first indulged in drugs and alcohol are feelings like fear, loneliness, peer pressure, and self-hate. I'm inclined to believe that if we took the time to look critically deep inside ourselves, we would find that we all possess a common, though strange, perhaps subconscious, disdain for who we have been.

As I've sought to confront and deal with the issues which are very instrumental to my continuing recovery, I had to openly admit first of all that I didn't care for who I was back then. I also had to admit that I hadn't given myself the chance to get to know who I really was, because I was trying to live up to what I thought others expected me to be.

The struggles which confront us during an extended period of incarceration are many indeed. But foremost for me has been that struggle to relive the chaos and self-destruction of a past which I'd just as soon forget in order to get in touch with who I was and am. My struggle has been to be alone with myself, to get to know myself, and ultimately come to love myself.

As I do this, I'm regularly surprised to discover some unique, overlooked positive quality which makes me feel good and hope-filled about who I am today and who I'll be in the future.

◆

Ronnie G., Nottoway Correctional Center, Virginia
Second degree homicide
9 years

IN RECOVERY, I'VE been looking at myself on the inside, trying to find myself and say what I always wanted to say. To do so, I started to apply the Twelve Steps in my life. A.A. has given me a new life, and for that I want to help others in recovery.

I've been in recovery for some time now, and I thank my Higher Power for the strength that helps me get through each day. Because I can't do this on my own, I must look to a Power greater than myself for guidance and comfort through this new way of life.

I take my hat off to all my friends in A.A.

◆

Bobby H., Branchville Training Center, Indiana
Reckless homicide
8 years

SEPTEMBER 2

I WAS TOLD most of my life that I wasn't a bad kid, but I didn't believe it. Besides, I wanted to be a "bad boy." I hung out with the older group all the time. It was with them that I took my first hit of pot, LSD, and drink of alcohol.

I was a searcher, looking for companionship. I couldn't find it at home, school, or anywhere else until I started doing drugs. I finally found what I wanted, but looking back on it now, I can see that I found it in the wrong place.

I've been in and out of lock-ups most of my life because of the drugs I was taking and selling. Since being in prison, I've learned that I could find companionship in N.A. and A.A. programs. I now work the Steps to recover.

I just thank my Higher Power for opening my eyes at the age of 16, which is how old I was when I came to prison, because now I'm truly free. I may be in prison, but I'm sober. And that is all that matters.

◆

Lawrence Y., Branchville Training Center, Indiana
Battery
5½ years

PRISON CAN HAVE a very sobering effect on those who have been incarcerated because of a drug addiction that resulted in criminal activities. It is not an alternative that I recommend if other options are available. But for many of us who are drug-dependent, incarceration could prove to be a liberating experience if the time is wisely spent.

I'm not saying that prison is the land of opportunity, but it can offer treatment possibilities for those who need help with their drug problem but may not have access to it on the streets. It is purely a matter of using our time in a productive and positive manner, to help ourselves by taking advantage of the various drug programs available. So don't let others who could care less about their own health and well-being pressure or dictate how you should spend your time in prison.

For the most part, people who continue to use drugs and refuse help are going nowhere, and there is nothing they would like more than to drag you down with them. After all, misery loves company. We can't afford to allow the false glamour of drugs to keep us down. In treatment, we can start our lives anew, and we may also end up helping someone we know and love become a drug-free person.

◆

Jon S., Louisiana State Penitentiary, Louisiana
Aggravated robbery, Aggravated burglary, Car theft
231 years

September 4

MANY PEOPLE VIEW drug use as a form of social entertainment and an alternative to having to face reality. But in truth, drugs numb our sensitivity toward ourselves and others while distorting our concept of what is truly important until we no longer care about anything other than supporting our habit.

Let's face it, using drugs isn't "cool" because there is nothing cool about destroying your life or being a part of that which destroys others. Yet each of us has the option to either be a part of the problem or a part of the solution.

Benjamin Franklin once stated, united we stand, divided we fall, an adage coined because he, as well as others, understood that the real enemy of this country would come from within and attempt to divide the unity that this nation was built upon and needs to survive. And even though this country has other problems that need to be addressed, let's not allow those problems to become excuses for avoiding the problems that drugs have created. Let's not permit drugs to control and destroy our lives, our families, and our communities. This is a problem that involves us all. If we want to survive as a nation, we must become part of the solution. And that in itself should be a goal that all of us feel is truly worth standing united for.

Jon S., Louisiana State Penitentiary, Louisiana
Aggravated robbery, Aggravated burglary, Car theft
231 years

A PRACTICING ADDICT has excelled in many areas: he is a salesman, confidence man, perfect liar, illusionist, pickpocket, scam man, thief, stool pigeon, organizer, and perfectionist. He has used his abilities to their fullest. In his zeal to feed his addiction he has used parts of his brain that other people normally don't use. The addict is a refined survivor and has subconsciously developed coping skills. The trouble is drug addiction.

Recovering addicts can be a "gift to the people." A recovering addict will do as good or better in any job than someone who has not been shaped by the challenge of overcoming drug addiction. He can spot a liar and a thief a mile away. He can tell if someone is sincere or not. Some employers have recognized that a recovering addict is a person who will excel in a work setting. But not all companies embrace them. We need more role models to set the pace in the general public. We need recovering people who can go to a job and make a difference in a positive way.

We can be a gift to society and to our employers. We know what pain is like, so we know how to love. We can become a gift to our family and loved ones. During our incarceration, God relieved us from our addiction. He gift-wrapped us with treatment. And when we're ready, He will release us.

Julian B., Cook County Jail, Illinois
Burglary
1 year

SEPTEMBER 6

FEAR IS A natural part of everyday life, but for the addict or recovering person, fear becomes more magnified. Will I make it through this next high? Am I going to maintain my newfound sobriety? Should I disclose anything about my past? How will people view me?

Fear brings on unwanted shame. I have a tremendous fear of failure. Fear makes me maintain a certain image of myself. I don't want people to see me at my weak point. I forget that most people have the same fears. I will adjust the volume of my fear so that I can hear them. Soft or loud, they must be addressed.

◆

Winston W., Counselor, Graham Correctional Center, Illinois

BEFORE I STARTED my recovery, I depended on external things for my happiness. This dependence offered only temporary satisfaction. Soon after obtaining my object or drug of desire, I was left once again with a deep void, which set me off again to try and validate myself through some other chemical high or materialistic gain. "If only" was often my rationalization for feeling so empty: if only I had more money, alcohol, drugs, or power.

In retrospect, all my answers were to be found within, for within me is an unlimited spiritual resource. But, like a dark cloud shrouding the radiant sun, I shut myself off from this bountiful source of power with greed, resentment, hatred, and other character defects.

Today, having had a spiritual awakening, I have cleared the way for the light of the spirit to shine. Even in prison, stripped of almost all my worldly possessions, I abound with joy and happiness. Through working the Twelve Steps, I have finally begun to find serenity.

◆

Richard K., Branchville Training Center, Indiana
Conspiracy to sell cocaine
8 years

SEPTEMBER 8

SOME OF US in prison get into a recovery program just to get an earlier out date. We refrain from using alcohol and drugs only because we don't want to lose any good time served. But recovery is not just about refraining from alcohol and drugs or an early out date. It's about restoring my heart, soul, mind, values, and self-respect.

When I first got into a recovery program it was for the courts and my family. After relapse and coming to prison, I made a remarkable discovery about recovery: I can only honestly have it for myself, not for the courts or my family or anyone else. I had to make the choice for myself: recovery or death.

After grasping the Twelve Steps and the program, I discovered that my problem wasn't other people or my everyday concerns, but how I responded to them. I found that addiction had imprisoned my emotions, my feelings, and the ability to be totally honest with myself and reality long before I saw any prison bars.

Today I know that being totally honest with myself is a major part of my recovery, but it takes working the Twelve Steps in my everyday life to make recovery possible, even in prison.

◆

John B., Branchville Training Center, Indiana
Sale of a controlled substance
10 years

I USED DRUGS to live and lived to use. Today I no longer have to live that way.

There was a time when I would spend all my money on cocaine and then have to turn a trick or fight with my children's father for money. I would stand on the corner selling soap or drywall shavings as cocaine.

Thank goodness, today I do not have to use to live or live to use. Today I have a Higher Power. I live by His will, not mine.

◆

Denise C., Cook County Jail, Illinois
Attempted murder

SEPTEMBER 10

A KEY FACTOR in recovery is acceptance. Once we learn to accept ourselves and our situation, we can begin to live free. Page 449 of the A.A. Big Book says it all.

> And acceptance is the answer to all my problems today. When I am disturbed, it is because I find some person, place, thing, or situation — some fact of my life — unacceptable to me, and I can find no serenity until I accept that person, place, thing, or situation as being exactly the way it is supposed to be at this moment. Nothing, absolutely nothing happens in God's world by mistake. Until I could accept my alcoholism, I could not stay sober; unless I accept life completely on life's terms, I cannot be happy. I need to concentrate not so much on what needs to change in the world as on what needs to be changed in me and in my attitudes.

I don't like being in prison, but I have accepted it. I didn't like myself or what I saw when I looked in the mirror. But I did something about it. I may not be free, but I am happy most of the time. I just have to recognize what has me disturbed and look it right in the eye and say, "This is how it is, and I can deal with it."

◆

Tom H., Moberly Correctional Center, Missouri
Sale of a controlled substance
20 years

WE HAVE ALL given up plenty to keep old King Habit happy. Most of us have given up a job, a home, our families; some have even given their life. I gave up my freedom, but it beats any graveyard in town. I thank God for the second chance He gave me for a real life.

There are certain things we must be willing to do to stay clean. Can we admit we are powerless over drugs and alcohol? Are we ready to turn our will over to the care of a Power greater than ourselves? Are we tired of lying to ourselves and our families? Are we ready to change our lives?

It's hard to imagine life without drugs and alcohol. What will we do for fun? We will have to find new friends and new playgrounds. We have to change our behavior. If we don't change our behavior, we can't expect a better life or freedom from addiction.

I've been clean and sober for almost three years. It's not always easy or a bed of roses, but I'm happy most of the time. I've got a new outlook on life. I'm a winner, not a quitter!

The bottom line is that we do have a choice. The only requirement is that we are honest with ourselves and really want to change.

◆

Tom H., Moberly Correctional Center, Missouri
Sale of a controlled substance
20 years

SEPTEMBER 12

LOOKING INTO MYSELF I see, feel, and act like a totally different person because of my new experiences in recovery. I now see a world of different opportunities, and I allow myself to feel better about who I am. And the action I take leads me to help others in their struggle with addiction.

The person I have become has been introduced to a life full of challenges. I have hope for the future, and my faith has been restored beyond explanation.

◆

Don M., Moberly Correctional Center, Missouri
Murder
20 years

GOD IS THE foundation of my recovery. The spiritual part is the essence of a working program for me.

I don't have to have all the answers today. I don't have to understand or be perfect. I just have to believe that God understands me, and providing I make the effort, He will reveal His will to me. I make the effort and leave the results to God.

Today I have a choice. I don't have to use. Upon awakening I ask God to allow me to stay clean just for today. This relieves me from fear of the future and allows me to focus on the moment at hand. To ask for freedom from self is to allow the sun to shine within my spirit. To exercise this is a decision and a freedom, a choice, a chance for change.

◆

Dennis R., Moberly Correctional Center, Missouri
Sale of a controlled substance
20 years

SEPTEMBER 14

I CREDIT MY success in recovery to learning the principle of detachment. One has to learn to detach from all elements that fuel an addiction.

It's often very painful, for some of those detachments could be from loved ones, lifelong friends, or even the area you grew up in. Still, the hardest of all is the detachment from your addiction.

◆

John S., Moberly Correctional Center, Missouri
Possession
10 years

BEFORE COMING TO the Fellowship of Alcoholics Anonymous, I was totally dependent on people, places, and things to bring me happiness and self-worth. But I have discovered the best source of emotional stability is obtained through my Higher Power. Dependence upon my Higher Power's perfect justice, forgiveness, and love is healthy. It works where nothing else can.

God, please keep me clean, sober, and free of all unhealthy addictions today.

◆

Les W., Moberly Correctional Center, Missouri
10 years

SEPTEMBER 16

WE OFTEN LOOK at a person who is out of touch with themselves and feel badly for them. But have we ever considered what drove them to that point? If we don't know what problems they are facing or how hard it may be, then how can we understand what they are experiencing? It's always much more than what meets the flashing eye.

As a peer counselor of substance abusers, I've learned that we must come together to solve our problems. We've got to replace our judgments with love and understanding, and apply the science of setting an example in acts and deeds.

As a recovering addict, I'm committed to making a change. This program has taught me to know myself like I've never known myself before.

◆

Andre H., Moberly Correctional Center, Missouri
12 years

ON THE STREET you can associate with whom you choose and attend any meeting that meets your recovery needs. But when you're in prison, you don't have the choice of who you live with or who you sleep beside. So you're forced to deal with personalities that you might not choose to associate with on the street. In prison you might have to deal with several hundred different personalities every day. And you may only have one or two meetings available to you.

At first I thought this was a real disadvantage to my own personal recovery, but in time I learned that it only strengthened my program and made my recovery more solid. I had to look the issue of "principles before personalities" dead in the face. I couldn't run to another meeting or get up and leave because I didn't like the person sitting beside me. I learned to accept him. It helped me become more understanding of him and of myself, because we are both dealing with recovery no matter what either of our personalities are like. I call it getting humble and putting my pride to the side.

I've found that on the streets or in prison you have to get involved and work the Twelve Steps before you can honestly meet any of your needs in recovery.

◆

John B., Branchville Training Center, Indiana
Dealing in a controlled substance
10 years

RECOVERING IN PRISON is not an easy path, especially for a four-time ex-con who knows all the dealers and users in the walls. But there came a point in my life when I had to ask myself, "Is this the way I want to spend the rest of my life?" When I could honestly answer "No," I was ready to look into this recovery thing.

I didn't know how to stay sober so I had to look for some help. I found it by going to the weekly A.A. meetings and reading and talking to the few other inmates who were interested in recovery. I found it in the concept of turning my will and my life over to the care of God, as I understand Him. Man, that was great, learning that I didn't have to be in control any longer.

But the problem was, prison life was not conducive to recovery. At times, there was a constant influx of negativity. I had to remove myself from that as much as possible. To do that, I turned to meditation and prayer.

I learned to look for the good in the people around me and to be thankful just to be alive because my actions outside of prison indicated I should be dead.

Today I have a responsible job working with incarcerated addicts and alcoholics. I have people in my life who care for me and I for them. The program is what it took for me to come into closer contact with my Higher Power, and I owe my life to it.

Steve C., Texas Department of Corrections
Theft, Drug charges, Robbery
On parole after 11½ years served

MY EXPRESSION OF anger has always been a major hazard for me. When growing up, I was always told that I should be "good," and good boys don't get angry. As I got older, my anger got me in trouble so I stuffed it. I drank and used to avoid feeling the anger I had.

Once I started going to prison, the exhibition of anger caused trouble in other ways. To show anger toward another in prison usually has one of two results: either there is a fight or you get locked up. Since I wanted to avoid both of those situations, I stuffed my anger even more until I was released. Then I resorted to chemicals to blunt my feelings.

The program teaches me I don't have to do that anymore. I can release my anger in appropriate, healthy ways. I'm able to identify some of the reasons for my anger and pain, which for me are the same feelings in different forms. I know that I was hurt in many ways as a child, things over which I had no control.

I don't have to put up a front any longer. I don't have to be the tough, uncaring person who needed no one and who didn't care if anyone needed him. I know that whatever I do is okay so long as I turn to my Higher Power for guidance. I'm a whole human being who has many God-given emotions, and I don't have to deny or be ruled by any of them.

◆

Steve C., Texas Department of Corrections
Theft, Drug charges, Robbery
On parole after 11½ years served

I REMEMBER WHEN I used to think that there was no hope for me, that drugs just had me defeated. I gave up on life until a friend of mine told me about the N.A. program. After being in one meeting, I knew that I was not the only person who had a problem.

The Twelve Steps of N.A. offer me a better way of living. I can look at myself in the mirror and tell myself that I love who I am, one day at a time. I know before I do anything that I have to be honest with myself. I have to have complete confidence in myself and know that the only way to help someone else is to help myself first.

Recovery is a lifetime thing. I have to continue to take personal inventory to make sure that I am doing the things that are right for me. I don't just stop getting high; I have to change my whole way of thinking and living. I have to internalize the important things that I hear in the meetings. I have to walk the walk as well as talk the talk. I have to know that I can win and accept that it is up to me to do so. I have to know every day that I am working on my recovery.

I say, if you want to recover, just go to N.A. or A.A. and be as open and honest as possible. Be willing to do whatever it takes. You can do it. I'll be praying for you. Remember, you are not alone.

◆

Kevin H., Staunton Correctional Center, Virginia
Distribution of cocaine
18 years

WHAT I DO with my life is a decision that ultimately comes from within. "Am I satisfied with the direction in which my life is heading?" and "Where will I be five years from now if I continue this self-destructive abuse of alcohol and drugs?" are but two questions I asked myself to begin the difficult journey toward a productive and meaningful life.

The first step is by all means the most difficult one; it's never easy for me to admit I have a problem. But once taken, I open myself to limitless possibility and potential. I can then begin setting small and reachable goals. Do I have a desire to earn my high school degree or learn a trade? If so, I contact my local community college or area vocational school and request information on how to enroll in their programs. If tuition is a concern, then I consider the financial assistance that is available. Opportunity is there waiting for me; if I take it, my life will be greatly enriched.

Common refrains among chemically dependent people are "No one cares," and "It's too difficult to let go of alcohol and/or drugs." But the truth of the matter, however brutal, is that no one in this world is going to be helped unless he or she puts forth the effort first.

The decision is mine. My life depends on it.

◆

Michael S., Louisiana State Penitentiary, Louisiana
Forcible rape
34 years

THERE IS NO way I would have ever said "I am an addict" if I wasn't in treatment at Taconic Correctional Facility. Being sober has allowed me to find and identify the real me, to change my attitude from negative to positive, to make decisions and choices.

I know that the only way I can achieve and maintain my goals and meet my responsibilities is by working the Twelve Steps day to day. I consider them tools for life. Hopefully, I'll become the responsible person I know I can be.

There is only one thing that has to receive my utmost attention, and that is the force of God. Without God I would not be alive today. It is indeed because of Him that I've been blessed to see and live so many tomorrows. I can feel God's presence within me, and I'm able to forgive people, places, and things from my past. Most of all, I can forgive myself and accept the things I cannot change, change the things I can, and pray for the wisdom to know the difference.

Thank God for recovery!

◆

Terry B., Taconic Correctional Facility, New York
Sale of a controlled substance
2½ to 5 years

ONLY AFTER DISASTER, after denial — "only after" — did I reach out to my Higher Power for help and put into action the tools of building a new life, first in my heart and then in my mind. I know it will be, one day at a time. But, in my case, it was "only after."

◆

Deborah J., California Institution for Women, California 16 months

WHEN I WAS a child, my dreams for the future didn't include becoming a drug addict. The future was mine. Great things were going to happen. Straight-A report cards, varsity sports, popularity — they insured this, didn't they?

Now I'm serving time because of my addiction. My husband is also in prison. My three children are wards of the state.

How did this happen? The drugs, money, cars, jewelry, guns? All the madness? I was powerless over an addiction, a disease. My addiction took me places I otherwise would never have gone. It tore me down.

Being arrested saved my life. I was broken, empty, confused, and lost. That's when my Higher Power came to me. That's when I was ready for His unwavering love.

Through education about my disease, I've acquired the tools needed to stay clean and sober. The joy is back in my life. Don't get me wrong, I'm still scared. But respecting my disease, knowing where it takes me, I can now step out into life.

My children will be mine again. My husband and I will reunite, a family once again. With God in charge, we'll remain forever free.

◆

Kimberlyn R., California Institution for Women, California
Possession for sales, Child endangerment, Weapons
3 years

I NEVER BELIEVED in drug treatment until I came to prison. This is my second time in prison, and I am proud to say I am blessed to be here. I thank God everyday for letting me see that I needed help.

In the drug program I learn about myself and who I am, inside and out. It's an educational recovery program. It's taught me that I am someone and I am important. It's taught me about my childhood and the problems that I never knew I had growing up. It's taught me to face situations head-on and deal with them.

I know I can't change the past but I can understand it, learn how to accept it, and make the present and the future better. The best thing I've learned is how to get in touch with my Higher Power. In my recovery, God is the most important part. In recovery, I've learned to love myself.

I am a new and special person. All my life I thought I didn't *get* enough attention; the problem was, I didn't *pay* enough attention.

◆

Estella O., California Institution for Women, California

SEPTEMBER 26

I'VE BEEN AN addict since I was 13 years old. I was a very defiant child, and being the oldest, I had greater responsibilities which I thought I took very seriously. My mother was also an alcoholic/addict, and we partied a lot together. We later started having a hateful relationship. I thought she expected too much from me, which made me even more defiant. I was soon using various drugs and had a family of my own, which I lost due to my addiction.

Now I'm learning to deal with my defiance and I'm doing so while locked up. I have a long road ahead of me. But there are people in my life who really love me, people I believed didn't love me. I'm clean today, for nine months now, and every day I work Steps One through Four. Without them, I couldn't be willing or accepting. N.A. — it works for me!

◆

Lisa S., California Institution for Women, California
Drug possession, Grand theft auto
3 years

I AM A rerounder. I had four-and-a-half years clean and sober, and slipped back into a world of broken promises and shattered dreams. I have learned some very important things. First and foremost, being clean and sober means I must completely change everything. I can't let my head tell me that I can still go around the same places and the same people. It doesn't work. I told myself I did not have to do what "they" did, but I was setting myself up. I should have made it a point to stay away from slippery places.

When I first got clean I began to sell drugs, thinking I could do this successfully. This was crazy thinking. I later learned that I wasn't really working my program, although I attended 30 meetings a month and was of service whenever I could be. But I was not working the Steps. Had I really been working the Steps, the thought of being a drug dealer would have been eliminated immediately.

◆

Starr D., California Institution for Women, California
Possession for sale
3 years

SEPTEMBER 28

I NEVER THOUGHT in all my years that prison would be any good for me. But I can honestly say that I am thankful for this trip through. In court I recall the judge saying I was to attend Alcoholics Anonymous and Narcotics Anonymous meetings. Then I was being endorsed for the drug treatment program. Following that, classification verified that I would be in the program four hours a day, Monday to Friday, and also work. Little did I know what the system had in store for me.

So now here I sit in the system, in the program, going to program meetings every day for four hours and working. I've learned a lot about myself and why I've done the things I've done. But most of all I've learned the past is the past and I can beat this thing called addiction, that seems to have so many of us crippled. I'm not alone. I'll take it one day at a time and ask God to continue to light the path I've chosen to follow.

◆

Terri T., California Institution for Women, California
Possession
16 months

I WAS THINKING to myself a few days ago that it's a shame for a person in prison to feel as good as I do. It's almost like I felt guilty for having a good outlook on life. I suppose there's a part of me that feels I'm here solely for the purpose of being punished, and that I'm not supposed to enjoy life while doing life.

But it's *not* a shame to feel this good in prison. Through recovery and much hard work, I've earned this attitude of gratitude toward life. My recovery has been a blessing. I've begun to fully recover what belonged to me years ago and was lost.

◆

Bud C., St. Clair Correctional Facility, Alabama
Murder
Life

September 30

ALL IS CALM now. Tired souls are once again put to rest. What will tomorrow bring? For some, a step forward. For others, another stressful prison day. A step back. We are like little children carefully being watched by people who care, while others just see us as problem children, wondering what mess we will get into come sunrise.

The moon and stars are out. Will there be a tomorrow for some of us? Only "time" will tell.

◆

Jackie V., California Rehabilitation Center, California
Burglary

WHEN DOES THE pain go away? Will I ever be really happy in my life? Can I really let the past die?

I feel I can make it, even if on my own. I've learned so much and on the inside I've grown. This is my life. I'm taking control, making a stand. Whether I am believed is neither here nor there. I'm going to make it, one way or another. One day at a time.

◆

Jackie V., California Rehabilitation Center, California Burglary

OCTOBER 2

WASTED. WASTED. My body, my mind, my life. That was my condition while on drugs. What was I thinking? What was I feeling? I felt plagued, tortured, lifeless, haunted. I didn't want to feel. I wanted to escape. So I attempted to deaden myself with drugs. I pretended not to hurt. But after the drugs wore off and I was denied more, I felt pain again. I was flooded with emotions and a new-felt pain of awareness. An awareness and a longing for a life free of bondage — free from drugs.

Although I'm an addict and I'm in the unfortunate and sad setting of prison, it does not make me a lesser human being. I know I have good intentions, and I'm still capable of giving and receiving love. I just have to follow through on those good intentions and show others my love and my worthiness.

Mainly, I must continue to love myself and have faith that I can succeed. The program has taught me that I can do this.

◆

Cynthia M., California Rehabilitation Center, California
Petty theft with priors

I'M USUALLY MY own worst enemy.

I admit to being a "Heckle and Jive" type person while on drugs, but who isn't? The thing is to accept who we were and who we are now. When we aren't beating ourselves down with guilt, remorse, or resentments, our good self, the one with heart, thrives in life.

I want to let the metamorphosis take place. I want to shrug off the hard exterior cocoon. I want to get unstuck from the old life and old ways and free my wings. Expand them, try them. I may be surprised at what I can do.

After trying on a new image and playing the part of "new-straight," of putting myself in new situations and new experiences, I became more comfortable and then more confident. Some people say, "Fake it until you make it." It was one of the tools that helped me.

◆

Cynthia M., California Rehabilitation Center, California
Petty theft with priors

OCTOBER 4

BEING BOTH AN alcoholic and sexual offender, Step Four is a special challenge in recovery: "Made a searching and fearless moral inventory of ourselves." I've found that both alcoholics and people with sexual issues have cycles of inappropriate thinking and feelings. I was an alcoholic long before my sexual dysfunction became apparent, and now as I try to identify and analyze this cycle of sexual insanity, I find it is indeed like a puzzle.

In treatment, we place a lot of emphasis on the group process. I'm in three different groups: A sexual issues group, a dysfunctional homes group, and a home place circle. But the constant in all these groups, for me, is Step Four. It's the Step that has helped the most.

So the special challenge I find in recovery is taking the tools and information — and the feedback that I receive from others — and working a program out for myself that includes an honest inventory of my actions. The other constant is, of course, the help of God.

◆

Frank F., St. Clair Correctional Facility, Alabama
Attempted rape
30 years

I HAD A good job for 20 years, nice family, good home — everything that an average working person could want.

Then one day I met someone who introduced me to cocaine and showed me how fast money could be made taking it from place to place. In turn, I introduced cocaine to people who I knew at work. I got to be known as someone who always had it.

Whenever I would see special programs on T.V. about people who used cocaine and hear what they would do to get it, I'd think, "Why don't they get a job and clean themselves up?" I was always putting them down. But when they came to me with their food stamps, rent money, and jewelry that was stolen either from home or a stanger, I took it no matter what.

But I was caught, and I've been down almost three years now. While at another facility, I heard about a substance abuse treatment program. All I saw was getting out in six months. I did not see myself as a drug addict. But being in the program I see that I am. I'm the same as the people I sold to, and I helped contribute to their addiction. This is a lesson that I feel deep within me. I'm glad the program was there to help put me back on the right path.

◆

Hattie R., Taconic Correctional Facility, New York

OCTOBER 6

I STARTED OUT on pot and beer. I liked the way they made me feel. My addiction progressed. I was using more and more each day till I wasn't getting the high I wanted. I started searching for a more potent drug, and so began my self-destruction.

Cocaine. Heroin. A drug-addicted baby. Abusive relationships. Crack. With crack, my insanity progressed so fast that I was doing crazy things for a one-minute high. I started going to jail. It seemed like every time I turned around I was being locked up. And then I got a state bid for a sale of crack.

In and out of prison for the next few years, I finally got sick and tired of drugs and going to jail. I got help for my addiction, but I didn't turn my will over to a Power greater than myself. I relapsed and ended up with another state bid. Because I was in a program I thought I was okay as long as I didn't use, but all the while I was relapsing. I wanted to do it my way, but I found out the hard way that I couldn't stay drug-free that way.

Today I'm fully dedicating myself to my recovery and to dealing with my mistakes and faults. I can honestly say that I'm happy with myself. And I can accept a lot of things that I couldn't deal with before.

◆

Adrienne C., Taconic Correctional Facility, New York

HERE'S HOW IT went for me. I met a girl who introduced me to drugs. I started trying all kinds of drugs and I didn't know how to handle it. I became an addict so fast it made my head spin, and I mean spin, because the things I valued most in my life just weren't important any more. I wanted it all to end, but I didn't know how. I even got shot and stabbed over drugs, but that didn't stop me. It was hard working out there, but I thought I had it made.

One day I went to work knowing I was going to get caught. Sure enough, they caught me and took me in and hit me with some time. I knew treatment was the only thing that could really help me.

I was willing in the beginning, but then as I started feeling my recovery I got scared, and I truly thought about giving up. But I looked back at my past and thought about the hell my life was in, and that scared me even more.

I need this recovery. I want this recovery. So I've stuck by it. And you know something? I've gotten in touch with myself, and I found out that I am a beautiful' person when I'm sober. I feel good about my life today because I'm sure of myself and I know I'm going to make it. I just have one thing to say about the recovery program: It's the best thing that's happened to me.

◆

Rosa S., Taconic Correctional Facility, New York

OCTOBER 8

IT WASN'T UNTIL I started getting sent to jail that I began to realize I was destroying my life with drugs. But my resolve to quit only lasted till I was out of jail and on the streets again. I thought I was so smart I could do things in a different manner. I was still too stubborn to realize how badly I needed help.

I kept coming back to jail for a few years until they finally decided to keep me. It took coming upstate to give in to my pride, come down to my senses, and get the help I needed.

I thank God for treatment programs like the one here at Taconic that showed me I am powerless over my addiction and that my life is unmanageable. They showed me how to open up to my true feelings. Humbling myself was kind of hard to deal with, but I learned to accept my weaknesses, and I am less defensive. I am at peace with myself today. I can admit my mistakes, but I don't fault myself because I am not perfect. I discovered that I can be a responsible and honest individual. This change has affected my relationship with others. I am not the same person I used to be. And I'm grateful.

◆

Luisa G., Taconic Correctional Facility, New York

BEING IN JAIL and in treatment doesn't mean people are always going to appreciate my recovery. People are going to re-act in certain ways — sometimes negatively — if they see a person changing. When that happens, it's up to me to have patience and not let myself get upset.

That is one problem I am working at on a daily basis — how to understand other people's actions and feelings. Sometimes I've caught myself getting very upset with certain individuals and I don't like the feeling. After analyzing the problem, I came to the conclusion that I have to be understanding and learn how to forgive myself and others and accept the things I cannot change.

One tool I've learned is to talk to the individual about the matter. After the discussion I feel a whole lot better. I also feel respect for myself for making the effort. I try my best, and I put my all into every situation or task that is good for me.

◆

Luisa G., Taconic Correctional Facility, New York

OCTOBER 10

YOU KNOW I never thought I would be saying this, but I am grateful for who I am today and for my new beginning in life. I took many things for granted at one time and that caused me a lot of pain and misery. So I am still learning not to let my guard down because it may cause me to fall back into an irresponsible way of behaving.

I am afraid to live that unhappy life again, being rejected by others because of my negative ways and seeing my goals go down the drain. So as I live day to day, I am trying to assure myself that I can do whatever I attempt to do, and if it doesn't come out right today, tomorrow is another day and another new beginning.

◆

Luisa G., Taconic Correctional Facility, New York

I AM READY today to fight off whatever may stop me from growing. I thank my Higher Power every day for giving me a second chance in life. I have turned my will over so He can give me the strength to deal with every situation that comes my way. I couldn't do it on my own before, and today I am not afraid to ask for help.

I used to act like I knew what life was all about, but all in all, I didn't know anything. I'm trying not to be phony because that's not me. I am going to be honest and happy. Everything that was meant to be will be as long as I am true to myself and love myself the way God made me.

I am proud of who I am. And I am grateful to the souls who discovered recovery.

◆

Luisa G., Taconic Correctional Facility, New York

OCTOBER 12

AT THE AGE of 29, I smoked base to see what everybody was raving about. I liked the way I felt after taking that first hit. After that day, I spent more and more time and money smoking base. I did things I'm ashamed of to get money to buy base. I ripped people off and stole from my family. I left my children with my husband to go off at night and meet people to buy base. I would go for two and three days just getting high, not caring whether he was worried or not. My whole life revolved around this drug. It wasn't until my arrest that I finally realized what I was doing to myself and my family. It took the fact that I was facing years in a state penitentiary for me to stop and say, "That's it!"

The day finally came when I was sentenced to two-to-six years in a state penitentiary. When I got there I was told what I needed in order to make my board, which wasn't until some 17 months later. I heard about a treatment program being held inside the prison. I was told to go to these meetings. I was cool with that until it came down to actually going to the meetings.

It wasn't until I got here that I realized how strong my disease was, and that I hadn't been myself for a long time. Dealing with my anger and hurt is a whole new experience for me, and I love that I am getting the help to recover from the disease of addiction.

◆

Deborah P., Taconic Correctional Facility, New York

TODAY I CAN say I like who I am and who I am going to be in the future. I don't look back at my yesterdays because they are over with. I am living one day at a time.

I thank my Higher Power, because recovery is my road to success. I know this time around that I am going to make it. I can be the kind of mother I long to be to my children. I have a wonderful life ahead of me, one that I shall accomplish in recovery.

◆

M.R., Taconic Correctional Facility, New York

OCTOBER 14

AS A FREQUENT inmate of the state penal system, I always made plans on how I was going to change "once I got out." I would figure out what I had done wrong and make vows to do things differently. But, what do you know, I kept finding myself back on the road to the penitentiary.

Finally, on my fourth trip to prison, I made the decision that I really did not want to live my life this way, but I knew that if I continued to use and drink the results would always be the same. So I started going to the A.A. meetings on the unit and reading the literature and talking to people who were doing the same.

The important thing is I did not wait until I got out again before making the necessary changes. I would be fooling myself if I thought I could wait until I walked out that gate to learn to live life one day at a time.

So I learned to practice the program and not focus on the negatives that permeate prison life. My Higher Power gave me each day to do with as I wished, and I chose to practice the principles of the program as best I could. The time until my release was spent learning acceptance, meditation, and searching for personal growth. I found it much easier to face life on the outside carrying the tools of the program with me.

◆

Steve C., Texas Department of Corrections
Theft, Drug charges, Robbery
On parole after 11½ years served

As a PRACTICING addict, I had many regrets about my past. I so regretted the pain and suffering I had brought upon myself and my loved ones, not to mention the victims of my crimes. I felt real bad and real guilty about many parts of my life. But while I was drinking and using I could do nothing about it. My pain and my guilt were justifications for me to continue doing what I was doing.

In recovery, I have a way to deal with my pain and my guilt. The program tells us we need to be willing to make amends to those we have hurt. I had said I was sorry many times before, but my apologies held no meaning if I never changed.

As a recovering person and an ex-inmate, admitting my past addictive behavior has not been easy, but I know it is essential to my continued sobriety. I have to say to people, "This is where I was, here is where I am now." The promise that "we shall not regret the past nor wish to shut the door on it" holds especially true for us ex-offenders. No matter how far down the scale we have gone, our stories can help others. But mainly, we help ourselves when we accept our past for just that, the past. We acknowledge it and move on, one day at a time.

◆

Steve C., Texas Department of Corrections
Theft, Drug charges, Robbery
On parole after 11½ years served

OCTOBER 16

SOMETHING I ONLY "try" is bound to fail because "try" is a loophole I give myself — an excuse for personal failure. I can never "try" a recovery program; I can only commit fully to "do" the program, step by step.

To decide to do something is a powerful, yet simple choice. It is heroic. It does not mean I'll never feel fear or know loneliness. A hero is just as fearful of failure as a coward. But where a coward only tries to back away or run away, the hero will persist despite obstacles and feelings of fear. He or she makes a determined choice and goes for it, despite the odds. It is very possible that a hero actually has more fear and negative feelings. But a hero goes forward anyway, with a vision of a good outcome and a positive future.

A hero is not brash and stupid. Rather he or she is patient, resisting haste. In the end, one can only "do" or "do not." Those who "do" make up the small number who endure, gaining recovery and peace.

God, teach me to "do" with peace and inner joy today.

◆

Victor D., Graham Correctional Center, Illinois
Drug trafficking
6 years

LEARNING TO SMILE in prison is as difficult for an inmate as learning to walk is for a baby. Halting steps, stumbling, falling, often getting hurt. But while the baby will keep up its attempts to walk and eventually succeed, many incarcerated people give up, and more still never even attempt to learn to smile.

The smile I speak of is not a mask, but a smile of inner peace and joy. I'm not talking about happiness that depends on "happenings," but joy which is the inner smile of peace; the manifest smile of an inner serenity that only contact with a Higher Power can produce. It's a smile of the inner person — spiritual, deep, and consistent.

In active addiction, we learned to put up fronts and put on smiles like clown make-up. We were grotesque parodies of real humanity. We were like clowns, but there was no laughter. Now, as we work each Step and strip our masks, the fruit of knowledge is taking root in our souls and we're learning the inner smile.

◆

Victor D., Graham Correctional Center, Illinois
Drug trafficking
6 years

OCTOBER 18

NOW THAT I am clean, I am always concerned about the progress that I'm making. The program emphasizes progress and takes pains to point out that there is no perfection.

Being true to the program and to myself, I must take notice as to how I'm changing internally. I need to be aware of my level of acceptance, anger, tendency toward self-pity, and the strength of my faith. I need to remember that if I fall short, I am still worthy of a different life if I continue to work for it. Falling short does not negate the progress I've made. In a sense, we are already in possession of the perfection we are striving for. Our perfection comes in our commitment to progress.

To keep trying is all we're required to do.

◆

Michael M., Graham Correctional Center, Illinois
Attempted murder, Multiple robberies

I KNEW I needed help for my addiction because I wasn't adjusting to being incarcerated. I told the warden that I was a drug addict and that I wanted some help. Now that I'm participating in a substance abuse treatment program, I feel a lot better because I am learning how to confront my fears.

As far as God is concerned, He is my role model. God is who I look to as I struggle for additional sobriety. Also, I use other addicts as a power greater than myself, because they are very helpful when it comes right down to it.

If I had not been allowed to participate in a treatment program before I was released, the Department of Corrections would have had to keep my bed available, because I would have been back through the revolving door. You know, I have learned that I was not just addicted to drugs, which played a big role in my life, but also to money, women, the streets, friends, the fast life, the list goes on. But through recovery, I'm regaining my abandoned ideals.

◆

Kenneth M., Graham Correctional Center, Illinois
Burglary
7 years

OCTOBER 20

OUR ADDICTION CREATED chaos and disorder within us. Any time we used drugs, knowing what they do to us, our lives were unmanageable and chaotic.

Our recovery is a process of rebirth. In our recovery, we begin to rebuild our disordered lives. It is often painful, with many tears. Rebirth in recovery is a spiritual rebirth authored by our Higher Power. Each of the Twelve Steps are steps in the process.

◆

Victor D., Graham Correctional Center, Illinois
Drug trafficking
6 years

IF YOU WANT to change your life, a recovery program is the best place to start. The program has a lot to offer if you are willing to do what is necessary to make yourself a better person.

I was an addict for 25 years, and I never thought about a program until I went to jail and found out how powerless I was. My life was totally unmanageable and I felt the need to accept some treatment. My way was always the wrong way, and I realized that I had to let go and let God because I couldn't do it by myself.

I never thought recovery would be so wonderful, just staying clean and sober one day at a time. I try to keep it real simple for myself. God, help me stay clean and sober today.

◆

Robert A., Graham Correctional Center, Illinois
13 years

OCTOBER 22

I'M 20 YEARS old. I never thought I'd be an alcoholic
and convict. I was too young, too innocent. But I was
wrong. I am an alcoholic and a convict, but with the
help of the program, I'm becoming more aware of all
my actions. In treatment, I've done a lot of thinking,
changing, and goal setting. Now I'm at the point of
putting these things into action.

I will succeed!

◆

David H., Graham Correctional Center, Illinois
Aggravated battery
4 years

I KEPT REPEATING the same events, expecting the results to be different. From chasing illusions and dishonesty to fear and denial, I have lived the culture of my addiction for many years. I became part and parcel of my addiction. It molded an ungrateful man. I neglected my morals and took life and those around me for granted. I never gave myself a serious and honest chance to develop maturity or to recognize that life could be lived truly clean and free from a dependency on any mind-altering substances.

Now, through defeat, I can confess that being 21 years old doesn't constitute maturity. It is very difficult to confront my addiction. Regardless of my past, the people I hurt, the choices I made, I believe I suffered more than anyone.

If the hands of time can change, so can I. I owe it to myself.

◆

Anthony W., Graham Correctional Center, Illinois
Possession of a controlled substance

OCTOBER 24

WHEN WE AWAKEN and think "Oh, what's the use?" the answer can be found in our Higher Power. When we let our Higher Power into our lives, everything is of use. Being in prison can make us feel that life has turned on us. Let us turn on to life instead.

In my addiction, my life was one big conflict, hectic at best. There was no time for meditation or learning or growing, only time for confusion and pain. But now, within these prison walls, I have found some measure of what I sought so desperately through drugs — a meaning, a purpose, and a contentment with who I am. And for today, I'm okay.

The old prison saying "Don't do the time, let time do for you" has new meaning. No longer do I think, "What's the use?" Living life on life's terms has its own rewards. I can truly say God is doing for me today what I cannot do for myself.

◆

Martin K., Graham Correctional Center, Illinois
Retail theft
3 years

BEFORE I CAME to know recovery, I always wanted people, places, things, and alcohol to bring life to me. In recovery, I see that it's up to me to bring life to me. I know if I want a better life than the past, I must rebuild myself to help myself.

It's all up to me.

♦

Charles S., Graham Correctional Center, Illinois
Aggravated battery
5 years

OCTOBER 26

WHY SHOULD I follow rules in treatment? I should follow rules if I want what I came to treatment for — recovery. In the past I had problems with the "No violence" rule. But I need to follow all the rules to let new family members know how to work the program. If I don't, then others will think that it's okay to do their own thing.

If I don't learn to follow rules inside prison, most likely I won't follow them in the outside world. Rules are set up to get us back in tune with doing what we should do in order to make something out of our lives. The rules are not that hard to follow if I keep my mind on what I'm in treatment for — and that's to get back on top of my life.

Following the rules and working the program, I have been free of drugs for about eight months. If I get back into my old ways of thinking, I'll never find recovery. Following rules and doing what I know is right has kept me from losing my mind. I know now that I can do what people expect of me, and I have no doubt in my mind about that.

◆

Larry W., Graham Correctional Center, Illinois
Possession of a firearm
5 years

WHEN I WAS serving time, both in prison and on parole, it was an act of surrender. My alcoholic/drug addict/criminal way of life forced me to serve time (surrender) or die. I surrendered my will to God and to a new way of living with A.A., N.A., and other support. To me, to serve time means to commit myself to my recovery process. I owe this to society, my family, and myself.

I serve as my Higher Power's will unfolds. I don't always know what the bigger picture is. The first time I went up for parole, I had served two years of an eight-year sentence for armed robbery. I had done all the right things: G.E.D., no lock-ups, A.A. attendance, self-study, prayer. Still, I got a one-year set off. This was my Higher Power wanting me to serve deeper, longer.

Now 15 years later, I know that if I had been released from prison then, I would have relapsed big time. I had not served enough time to work a full recovery program. I needed more time to work the Twelve Steps, trust and find a Higher Power, help others, and really serve.

I thank God today. Prison, A.A., and a Higher Power have saved my life and given me a life. It works!

◆

Perry G., Maryland Department of Corrections
Armed robbery
Served 3 years; 5 years on parole

OCTOBER 28

MY PERSONAL EXPERIENCE as a client in recovery has been painful, but through the pain I have gained new strength. I experienced abuse as a child, and the child within was never able to grow. I numbed the pain with alcohol and drugs at a very early age. Dealing with my family's past and their dysfunctional behavior helped me realize that the abuse wasn't my fault.

Relapse is still possible, however. I have dealt with my family issues and cried through the pain, but after so many years of hard drug use, I find my wild, crazy and cunning addiction is still alive and waiting for me to shoot that first shot.

Today I'm alive, clean, and happy. Tomorrow has not arrived yet, but when it does, I will use God as my power to defend, protect, and bring me to the place He wants me to be.

Making new friends is important. Tell me the right things to do, encourage me, be by my side when I have a problem, and don't turn your back on me when I need you. And when I can't walk the mile, carry me until I'm able.

God's orderly direction is my new outlook. By seeking, I have found peace.

◆

Timothy S., St. Clair Correctional Facility, Alabama
Criminal solicitation
Life

MY ARREST, CONVICTION and incarceration were all a result of divine intervention. Had I been allowed to continue my insanity in the free world, I'm sure by now I would be dead. By the grace of God, I was restored to sanity and blessed with a total lifestyle change.

I found Narcotics Anonymous while incarcerated, and I began to work the Twelve Steps of recovery. I've been rescued from morning dope sickness, sweats and chills, cramps, and sleepless nights. By the grace of God I didn't take a fatal overdose, I didn't have a fatal seizure, I wasn't gunned down, I didn't develop HIV or AIDS, nor any of the many other horrible things that often come with the disease of addiction.

I believe in divine intervention and the spiritual joy it brings. It has allowed me to find myself and to live life drug-free. Because of God's divine plan and Narcotics Anonymous, I now have self-esteem, self-worth, self-respect, and self-love.

◆

Eddie S., Logan Correctional Center, Illinois
Possession of a controlled substance
8 years

OCTOBER 30

EVERY DAY IS a constant challenge to overcome what lies within me. My faith in God and my desire to change help me continue when I feel like giving up.

I've experienced more pain in recovery than in all my life. However, I've grown stronger by accepting the things I cannot change and sharing my feelings with others. It helps to know that someone cares.

◆

Ricky H., St. Clair Correctional Facility, Alabama
30 years

I WAS RAPED as a young man. The hardest part of my recovery is forgiving my attacker. I grew up hating the people who did this to me. But forgiving people is a big part of recovery.

The only way I was able to forgive was through developing my spirituality. Now my Higher Power plays a big part in my life. Without a Higher Power, I would never have been able to forgive.

◆

Billy T., St. Clair Correctional Facility, Alabama
Armed robbery
40 years

NOVEMBER 1

SINCE BEING IN recovery I have learned a great deal about goals and why I could never reach mine. When it comes to reaching my goals I am my own worst enemy. On many occasions I would set goals that were unattainable. Even when I set attainable goals, I would subconsciously sabotage any success I was about to reach. It seems that every time I had things going my way, I would do something stupid or make a wrong choice.

I have learned some very definite steps that I must take in order to reach my goals. First, I must write them down. Second, I have to outline my plans. The third step is probably the most important: I must take action. Finally, I must continue to evaluate my progress along the way.

Another thing that I must do is keep a positive mental attitude and believe in myself. I know that by maintaining positive self-talk and working the Steps, I can obtain any goal that I set for myself.

◆

Michael H., St. Clair Correctional Facility, Alabama
Rape

I STARTED SMOKING pot before I was 6 years old. My brother and his friends were always getting high and I enjoyed hanging around with them. When I was 11, I started shooting dope.

Naturally, things only got worse. I wasn't able to attend school regularly or learn anything when I did go. I didn't have a job and wasn't looking for one, so in order to support my habit, I stole from my family and anyone else that left anything within my reach.

This is my second trip to prison, and unless I recover, I will continue on this path.

As a part of my treatment I'm required to take on responsibilities and increase my education, but I'm also advised to look back at the early stages of my life and try to identify why and how I developed my addiction.

I'm learning to enjoy life and love myself just as I am.

◆

Jeremy F., St. Clair Correctional Facility, Alabama
Theft, Escape
15 years

NOVEMBER 3

WHEN I ENTERED the program, my outlook on life was the same as it had always been — negative. Now that I've learned the fundamentals of the program, I want what it offers me, which happens to be life itself, something I had lost sight of.

This is far from being an easy program. There are times when I feel like giving up, but I must stay with it and not lose sight of the fact that giving up on this program would be giving up on my life.

The program reminds me to be completely honest, open, and willing to admit how I feel and where I went wrong. It requires that I admit some very deep and painful personal problems which I felt I would never speak of for the rest of my life.

Spiritual power is very important in my recovery. With God, anything is possible.

◆

Willie T., St. Clair Correctional Facility, Alabama
Burglary
20 years

Before I enrolled in St. Clair's substance abuse program, I had no idea that I even had a sexual addiction. But after hearing other guys talk about their problems with sex addiction and learning the different ways such addiction can affect people, I came to realize that I did, in fact, have sexual issues. I decided I could either live with it or deal with it, depending on whether or not I wanted to be totally well.

To elaborate, when I was 11 years old, my older sister, in the throes of adolescence, used me as a practice device in order to learn how to attract and hold on to her boyfriends. I never had anyone to whom I could go to and talk about the guilty feelings I was having, so the activity continued off and on for two years. Plus I had to carry the guilt and the shame that came with it inside me for 28 years.

Now that I've identified the problem and discovered what the root of that problem was, I have been able to relieve my guilt and shame by talking about it in my home place circle. I have even begun to open up about it to my present wife to let her get to know me more intimately.

◆

Roger T., St. Clair Correctional Facility, Alabama
Burglary
50 years

NOVEMBER 5

I WAS ATTRACTED to alcohol because it gave me confidence to talk to any girl I wanted. I was kind of shy, but the more I drank the more I talked. Drinking also helped me socialize with friends. Sometimes I would find myself drinking to give me courage to be around certain people who I thought I wouldn't fit in with. I figured the more I drank, the more people I would meet.

I never realized I could meet people without drinking. Since I've been in treatment, I have met a lot of new friends, and I have learned that I can socialize without using alcohol. If people can't accept me for the person I am, then they are not my real friends. Real friends accept you as you are — not for who they want you to be. I can't worry about what other people think, I have to be the person I am. God is the only person I have to impress.

◆

Corbett W., Jester Unit I, Texas

IN MY RECOVERY I have learned how to control my anger by humbling myself and asking God to guide me and give me patience. Patience brings growth, and for me, it's also brought gentleness. God has helped me to control my anger by helping me to become more gentle. Now I'm clean and sober, and I plan to live my life on His terms.

◆

Frederick F., Jester Unit I, Texas
Assault

NOVEMBER 7

I ENTERED THE program as a skeptic. Little did I realize how glad I would be to be sober.

Once I was willing to listen, I learned to accept that I was not a bad person, that I was capable of loving and being loved, and that I could hold my head up and respect myself. Then I knew everything would be all right.

◆

Robert R., Jester Unit I, Texas

FEAR IS A four-letter word with a big meaning. Because I didn't know how to deal with it, I relapsed twice. I was fearful of my feelings and of dealing with pain. I knew about physical pain but not emotional pain, because to me, emotional pain could be covered up and forgotten' about. I thought as long as my pain didn't show on the outside, it didn't exist.

Without God, my Higher Power, I will always be afraid, hurt, and full of pain. All I have to do is let Him take over and my fear is gone. Thanks to God and this program, today I have no fear. As long as God is willing to take the fear away from me, I am willing to give it to Him. God is my answer to fear, and I start each day asking Him to remove it. And it works.

◆

Drek L., Jester Unit I, Texas
Burglary

NOVEMBER 9

RECOVERY TAKES TIME. We didn't become addicted overnight, and we won't recover overnight either. Many of us have deep-seated issues to deal with now that we no longer have our old solutions of alcohol and drugs to rely on. If we don't deal with these issues on a spiritual basis, we'll become like a volcano: sooner or later we'll explode.

It is so important to build recovery on a spiritual level, to open our hearts and minds to the concept of a Power greater than ourselves. And we must share how we feel with others. It was once said, "A problem shared is a problem cut in half."

But please remember: Take it a day at a time, a step at a time.

◆

Melvin L., Jester Unit I, Texas
1 year

HERE'S MY PRAYER to my Higher Power:

I admit and accept that I am powerless, that I have no control over my life, other people, or situations. I need your help to guide me and be my strength each and every day. Please keep me safe and free. Help me to learn to live with my past and to share it with others so that it may benefit them. Help me to accept my humanness. Take away my selfishness and liabilities so I can become closer to you and to other people.

Help me to find the people I've harmed and to repair the damage I've done. Help me each day to understand and be aware of my weaknesses and strengths, that I may help instead of harm other people. Teach me to be humble. Help me to constantly be aware of your will for me.

Allow me to offer hope and strength to others who suffer the pain of life. Help me to do what is right instead of needing to be right. Help me guide others to your way of life, so they, too, can find the peace of mind and calmness of heart I have found.

◆

Melvin L., Jester Unit I, Texas
1 year

NOVEMBER 11

SOMETIMES RECOVERY IS a hard process, and it can put us on a roller coaster of feelings every time a new day arrives. I'll use myself as an example.

There have been several occasions when I just wanted to pack up and go back to the g-yard because the pain of recovery was so unbearable and intense. I wanted to let it all go and keep running, just like I've done all my life.

I got to the point where I went and tried to get some pills and alcohol because I'd gotten in touch with some feelings I didn't want to deal with. The only thing that kept me from relapse was that the man I approached had quit selling, and I couldn't get to the other part of the compound.

Then again last night I was dealing with a problem about my daughter, and it had me scared and I came pretty close to getting up out of my chair and just giving up. But I've learned something from these ordeals. I've got some problems, but help is here for me. I need to overcome my desire to run away, because it isn't going to help matters any.

◆

Steve L., St. Clair Correctional Facility, Alabama
Robbery, Theft
25 years

I WAS REPEATEDLY raped by my uncle at the age of six for about a year. I hated it. I felt ashamed, angry, unwanted, alone, and mad as I grew up. I never trusted anyone until I started the substance abuse program here at St. Clair.

I'm 36 now, and people are helping me dig up those feelings and deal with them. This is very hard sometimes, and I'm still working my way through this. I know I have to do this work so it won't be passed on later in my life.

If I were to tell the readers something that would help them it would be this: Life is never simple. You must learn to quit stuffing feelings and let them out. Sometimes you can talk about it. Also you can write out your feelings.

I guess what I am saying is — deal with your problems and feelings. Learn who you are and what you are like because everyone is different. Think positively and sooner or later positive things will be a part of your life. You can only get out of something what you put into it.

◆

John C., St. Clair Correctional Facility, Alabama
Rape
30 years

November 13

It's a blessing to have a substance abuse treatment program in a maximum-security prison. This program helps me with my addiction and in all areas of my life. If I hadn't come into the program, I wouldn't have been able to deal with my past and the things that really bother me the most.

This program has helped me learn many things anew. Now I understand true self-love, where before I never did. I'm also able to admit that I am powerless over my addiction, when at one time I thought I had it under control. I can deal with my anger in a positive way instead of negatively. And I have built up my confidence and self-esteem.

One of my goals is to stay sober and clean whenever the time comes for me to go free. I want to go out in society and live a productive life.

You have to take risks in order to get help, and I took a risk in recovery. Fortunately, I found out that people here have some of the same problems I have. Recovery is the way for me. With my Higher Power, I know that I can make it.

◆

Lorenzo M., St. Clair Correctional Facility, Alabama
Murder
Life without parole

ALL MY LIFE I stayed around people who agreed with my way of thinking. I didn't want to see or hear anything new or different because I was comfortable with my old ways. I wouldn't have admitted it then, but the truth is I was scared of anything outside my way of life. I ran real fast from change.

I'd pick and choose who I would listen to. If I didn't like a person, he couldn't tell me anything about me or my actions. But in treatment, guys were not telling me what I wanted to hear, they were telling me what I *needed* to hear, and I wasn't comfortable with that at all.

Hearing how others really saw me started the process of recovery in my life. I hated it at first and still do at times. The key for me now is to stop blocking out what others say because I don't like their personalities or the way they express their opinions. Today I work real hard at looking at what is being said rather than who is saying it or how he is saying it.

Being told what I want to hear will not help me grow. If you have a friend in recovery, be honest about what you see. He may be mad at you for a while, but later on he will thank you for caring enough to tell it like it really is.

◆

James H., St. Clair Correctional Facility, Alabama
Murder
15 years

NOVEMBER 15

MY SPIRITUAL AWAKENING came when I finally surrendered my life to God and got out of my selfish behavior. As I really began to apply myself to God, I began to see numerous changes in my life take place.

My Higher Power means that I can now begin a new lifestyle, new behaviors, and I have a chance to right the wrongs that I committed. It also means that I don't have to rely on my own abilities anymore. I trust in God to meet my needs. Without my Higher Power, I cannot sustain a purposeful life.

It helps to know that God is leading and strengthening me so I can perform the Steps of a recovery program.

◆

Lawrence L., Jester Unit I, Texas
Felony theft

AFTER FOUR TIMES in and out of the prison system, I finally realized that my drinking had a grip on me and the only thing that could ever break the chain was to admit to myself that I had a problem. That took a lot for me to do, but I knew that if I didn't, I would always be in prison.

So I got down on my knees and surrendered all to God. I asked God to help me because I was powerless over everything. Now I have peace within myself. God works miracles, and I am one of them. The only thing that keeps me growing stronger is God.

God always answers prayers that come from the heart.

◆

Santos H., Jester Unit I, Texas
DWI

NOVEMBER 17

I'D LIKE TO tell you the story of my almost-fatal relapse. Like most of us, I was an extremely abusive drinker for most of my life, and, like a lot of us, I hit bottom. The only treatment I could afford was going to A.A. It does work; I know, because it worked for me for almost five years.

But I quit going to meetings and poured myself into work. One night after work, some of the guys asked me to join their poker game. Everything was going great. I was winning a little and enjoying myself. But every so often, somebody would offer me a beer. At first I kept refusing, but something in my head kept saying, "Hey, it's okay. You've been five years without a drink, your body is in great shape again." I decided a couple of beers might do me good.

I was wrong. Once I started, I couldn't stop. I went into a blackout. I woke up in the hospital and learned I had hit a parked truck at 60 miles an hour. I busted my ribs, split my head open, and busted a lot of facial bones. I almost bled to death.

I couldn't believe it. After five years of sobriety I now have a DWI and five years to think about it. I thank God and the judge for sending me to this treatment center. Friends, if you think this could never happen to you, please think again.

Leroy W., Jester Unit I, Texas
DWI
5 years

TO ONE WHO thought he had it all together, fear is a very cold and unforgiving feeling. Fear is with me every day. Fear of not waking up in the morning to see if God is going to let me make it yet another day in here. Fear of not knowing if I'm giving 100 percent of myself to my program. Fear of knowing that the very thing that put me in here is still out there waiting for me. The hardest thing of all is knowing that death and I have been walking hand in hand.

Now I'm putting back the pieces of my life with God, myself, and my family. I know that I have to give up certain things to get back in the stream of life. I need to use the tools that have been given to me, and I must be willing to admit to my Higher Power that I need His help. I hope never to see the insanity that lived in me come back to haunt my life again.

I am not very good at putting my feelings into words that make any sense to anyone but myself, but I will leave you all with this: Question not what God does in your life; seek only to understand.

◆

Luther W., Jester Unit I, Texas

NOVEMBER 19

I WAS SELF-DESTRUCTIVE from the day I took my first drink in the summer of 1973. I moved on to bigger and supposedly better drugs to resolve issues in my life I couldn't handle alone. I didn't stop until my arrest in October of 1992.

In January I arrived here not wanting to ever drink or drug again. I wanted to learn some tools for recovery so I could go back into society to live a normal life.

Treatment has a lot to do with repetition — doing things over and over. It's the same with the Twelve Steps of Alcoholics Anonymous. I will never ever finish them, because there will always be something to add as I grow and continue in my recovery.

Parkside/Gateway's Substance Abuse Treatment Center and the Governor of Texas have given me hope for a new life, and I will always cherish it.

◆

dward M., Jester Unit I, Texas

I WAS A person who thought I could control everything: my construction company, teaching school, and my naval reserve status. But crack cocaine had me whipped, and it controlled my life for years. If that's not powerless and unmanageable, I would like to know what is.

Fortunately, through all my defeat, I still have a family, my wife, two sons, and twin girls who love me even when things seem hopeless. Today I can give thanks to this program and work it to the best of my ability. Thanks to my Higher Power for leading the way.

◆

Edward M., Jester Unit I, Texas
Theft

NOVEMBER 21

I DON'T KNOW what caused my emotional problems or when they started, but it seems as if they have been with me all my life. I can't remember a time before this program that I had any sustained periods of happiness. My first memories were that something was wrong, but I was unable to put my finger on it or really describe it.

But what I lacked in happiness I made up for in fantasy. I always believed that happiness was just around the corner or over the next hill. I believed that when something changed, or I did something special, I was going to be happy. I chased this illusion for 40 years.

The world is full of publicity that tells us that romance is the key to happiness, so I had a go at that too. Although I enjoy romance, it did not remove the feeling that all was not right with me. I still couldn't find the key.

In the program I'm learning to communicate with others and to tell someone that they hurt my feelings. For the first time I'm learning what a true friend is. Although I may not solve all my problems, the program is teaching me the happiness that comes with empathy.

◆

Michael S., St. Clair Correctional Facility, Alabama
Assault
15 years

MY PROBLEMS WITH drugs started when I was 19 years old. I was engaged to the woman I wanted to marry, but we split up and I started drinking heavily. Drinking made me depressed, and my behavior led to arrests for public drunkenness and DUI. One night while drinking whiskey and smoking pot, a friend and I decided to pick up a prostitute. When we had trouble finding one available, we went to the home of someone my friend knew and we raped her.

After I got locked up I felt miserable for what I had done and tried to commit suicide. I didn't succeed. When I got into the prison system, I decided to search for the answers to why I did what I did.

I'm grateful that I'm now getting help, but it isn't easy. There's a lot to understand, and I can only do it one day at a time.

◆

Gary R., St. Clair Correctional Facility, Alabama
Rape
Life

NOVEMBER 23

I'VE ALWAYS LIVED from one minute to the next without any thought of the future and what it had in store for me. By not having any goals to work toward, I was always in situations that were self-destructive for myself as well as those around me.

In recovery, learning to set attainable goals has helped me find the right direction to take. Two years ago, my future became very important to me. If I hadn't set any goals, I would still be in the same situation I was in then.

I have learned the steps for setting short-term as well as long-term goals that are realistic. I can attain them a day at a time, as I live a productive life. With my goal-setting skills I've also developed a positive mental attitude. These are two great steps in my journey into re covery.

◆

e E., St. Clair Correctional Facility, Alabama
bery

THERE IS NO judgment that is as important or as potentially harmful as the judgment I pass on myself. My awareness of life has been real shallow. I was always looking for something to make me feel better, act better, produce more, not realizing I was blind to the harsh judgment that I passed on myself.

My addiction was like a death sentence. Waiting execution, I find myself wanting more out of life. What a sad, miserable ending my life could have taken.

Thank God I have awakened and realized that the judgment I pass on myself can be the chain that binds me or the spirit that sets me free.

◆

Robert J., St. Clair Correctional Facility, Alabama
Sexual abuse
10 years

November 25

PRISON IS WHAT it took for me to take a look at my life. After being here for more than three years and free from any mind-altering substances, I have been introduced to the real me. I've learned things about myself that I have neglected for a long time. I learned that I have emotional problems. I was ashamed of myself for not graduating with my class and for allowing peer pressure to overtake me. But most importantly, I've learned what to do about these things.

I believe in my heart that confinement and recovery are God's ways of saving me and giving me another chance to be someone. I've never wanted so badly to have to pay bills and have responsibilities. Now that I've taken the steps to prepare myself, to walk back into the world that defeated me, I will be ready and eager to meet the challenges that life has to offer. But this time I'll do it with a clear mind and heart. By doing so, I won't have to worry about coming back to jail because I'll be too busy doing the next right thing for all the right reasons.

◆

Walter O., St. Clair Correctional Facility, Alabama
Battery
8 years

THE GROWTH THAT we strive for in this program can only be accomplished by feeling the accompanying pain. How often have we heard the edict, "No pain, no gain?" It seems that nowhere is this more evident than in the process of recovery.

As practicing addicts and alcoholics, our lives were full of pain, but we spent most of our energies trying to cover it up. As convicted felons, we had the added burden of being looked at as societal outcasts who did not deserve to be thought of as feeling and caring human beings. Perhaps no one had those feelings about us more strongly than ourselves. Our addictions were fueled by the vicious cycle of shame, guilt, remorse, and self-recrimination.

The program tells us that we must experience the pain we've been carrying in order to have a chance at recovery. If we hold on to the pain, we are increasing our chances for relapse. As an inmate for 11 years in the state penitentiary, I learned to keep to myself and not let anyone know how I feel. As a recovering addict/alcoholic, I have learned that to hold on to the pain and not share it with another human being will kill me. So I share my pain and fears, and in doing so, I grow. It's this process of growth that helps me to stay sober.

◆

Steve C., Texas Department of Corrections
Theft, Drug charges, Robbery
On parole after 11½ years served

November 27

THE MOST POWERFUL recovery tool I have is acceptance. I accept myself for who I am, I accept others for who they are, and I accept that 99 percent of what goes on around me is out of my control.

As an ex-convict with four trips to the state penitentiary, I had trouble believing that I could ever be accepted in mainstream society. With the help of this program, the fellowship, and my faith in my Higher Power, I know that I am accepted as a valued human being, worthy of love, respect, and consideration.

My belief in myself is strengthened by recognizing my powerlessness and turning my will and my life over to God as I understand Him. It is much easier to accept people, places, and things when I know I am not in control. During my life as a practicing addict, I had to be in control of everything and everyone around me in order to get that fix or pill. Knowing that I am only along for the ride and that the outcome is in God's hands is part of what keeps me sober.

C., Texas Department of Corrections, Texas
Drug charges, Robbery
after 11½ years served

IN SOME WAYS I feel I'm very lucky to have had the experience of my drinking and drugging days. Some people in the program seem to have trouble remembering just where their using would ultimately take them. After a year or two of sobriety, they would think, "Hey, things are going pretty good for me now, I may be able to handle a drink or two." And they will go out and relapse. And while some people make it back into the program, others die before they have the chance.

I know where my using will get me: I'll end up back in the penitentiary. I know that if I pick up past behaviors, I will get exactly the same results.

My Higher Power has given me a reprieve, one day at a time. But the reprieve doesn't come without work on my part. It is contingent on actions that I take every single day. They are following the Steps and principles of the program and remembering to be grateful for the opportunities I have for life and growth.

I am grateful for the people God has put in my life, people who allow me to feel love and compassion for myself and my fellows and I'm grateful for the universe, and the green earth, the animals, and the sunset. I'm grateful that I'm able to feel God's presence in everything around me, if I but look for it.

◆

Steve C., Texas Department of Corrections, Texas
Theft, Drug charges, Robbery
On parole after 11½ years served

NOVEMBER 29

I AM GRATEFUL for my sponsor today because he guides me through the program. My sponsor doesn't tell me what to do, but he helps me work my program responsibly.

At best, my sponsor loves me when I love myself. He shares his experience, strength, and hope. He also shares the successes and failures in his own program. I have learned much from my sponsor's wisdom and love. I've learned to release the urge to run away from this new kind of loving relationship and begin a process of trusting another person.

In the past, there were people I couldn't trust. In order to stay sober and clean, I need to trust again. My sponsor happens to be an ex-con, which proved to be a major help. But I only get out of this relationship what I put in. This means taking the risk to ask questions, writing and calling him, speaking at meetings, and making daily contact.

God speaks through my sponsor when I'm open and ready to listen. Without my sponsor, I'm not sure I would still be sober.

◆

Perry G., Maryland Department of Corrections
Armed robbery
Served 3 years; 5 years on parole

DURING MY YEARS of addiction I blamed everybody and everything but myself for my behavior and for all the consequences of my behavior. I had an excuse for everything. I justified and rationalized everything that happened. Every time I went to prison, I blamed the snitches and the judge. Every time I went to lock-up, I blamed the prison guards. But during my last incarceration and while participating in a prison-based treatment program, I had to face the truth — I had no excuses and no one to blame for my condition but myself.

I'm thankful that during my recovery process, I woke up and realized that where I was in my life was not where I wanted to be — and I did something about it. I slowly began to learn from my mistakes, started taking action to make things better, and made the time to do the things that were truly important to me. The most important things then and now are my Higher Power and personal recovery.

Today, 12 years clean, I am totally convinced that the most powerful tools of successful recovery are responsibility and accountability.

Today, my recovery program is dependent on my willingness to be responsible and to hold myself accountable. When this stops, relapse is inevitable.

◆

Bob K., Drug Program Specialist
St. Clair Correctional Facility, Alabama

December 1

ONE OF THE first and most important steps I took during the process of recovery was surrender. When I hit bottom during my last incarceration for multiple felony offenses, I was treatment-ready and knew it was my last chance, so I approached it as a life-or-death situation.

I admitted to myself and others that I was powerless and my way of thinking had not worked. This was easy for me to recognize since my best thinking had landed me in prison.

I'm very thankful that the treatment program staff cared enough about me to tell me all the things I didn't want to hear about myself. Much of what they told me was that I had to surrender, and that is the truth that set me free. It was not easy, but I totally turned myself over to the recovery process.

Today I am a recovering addict with 12 years clean time and a list of outstanding achievements and contributions. It amazes me that I wasted years trying to beat the system, when today I am "beating the system" in a very positive and productive way. Following my own recovery process, I surrendered my life to the important mission of helping people who are locked away in penal institutions to surrender and free themselves from the self-destructive patterns of addiction.

◆

b K., Drug Program Specialist
Clair Correctional Facility, Alabama

I'M A REROUNDER, just coming back into recovery for the second time. While out in population I had time to think. Even though leaving the program was wrong, at the time it seemed to be the thing to do. After seven months of intense recovery, my emotions and feelings were so stirred up that I felt the need to bail out, go back to the old me. So much for a dope addict's judgment!

I thought I could handle it. I even told others in the program that I no longer felt like I needed the intense rigors of a therapeutic community. But as usual I was wrong. It didn't take long to find myself back in the same rut. Instead of feeling my feelings and working through them, I was medicating them. The results were the same as before.

Confinement poses many problems in addition to the ones we face in the streets, and medicating them only looks like an easy out. Now that I'm back in recovery, away from the negativity and the bedlam of population, I feel relaxed, I feel needed, and I want to achieve something better for myself and my family.

As a drug addict, I may crash and burn from time to time, but the main thing is to never give up. With my Higher Power's help, I'll make it, one day at a time.

◆

Mark A., St. Clair Correctional Facility, Alabama
Robbery
Life without parole

DECEMBER 3

THERE IS ONE thing I have learned about myself since being in treatment. All of my past convictions have been drug-related. So is the crime I'm now serving time for. And I was high when the crime was committed.

I have learned a lot in treatment, and I have been clean and sober for 21 months. Even though I once went eight years in prison without getting high, that experience taught me that spirituality is a very important part of recovery. Along with spirituality, I needed to learn about addiction and the root of my problems. I also need to be aware of warning signs that occur from time to time. No longer do I have to live a false life centered around fantasies and lies.

I'll be in recovery for the rest of my life. It's good to feel again, to laugh, to cry, and most of all, to deal with life's problems head on without cutting corners and taking shortcuts. Because of recovery I have a new life. No longer am I a part of the discarded material that society looks at as no good and dirty. Even in prison I have a good life, because within I'm brand new. My thinking is new. I have found the morals, principles, and values that my disease had taken away.

◆

Kenneth G., St. Clair Correctional Facility, Alabama
Robbery
Life without parole

I WAS RELEASED from prison in 1990 and I started back using drugs about six months later. I didn't get into trouble right away, but I felt I was losing control of my life and couldn't seem to change the way I was going. So I checked into a 28-day program and thought I had whipped my addiction because I hadn't used for 28 days.

But, faced with the prospect of dealing with the everyday problems of life sober, I quickly found out I wasn't able to handle it. One month after leaving treatment, I relapsed. This time it was worse than ever before. I had no control at all.

I found myself in bad situation after bad situation, with the law just one step behind. Things got so bad that I had no idea what to do. I thought maybe jail wasn't such a bad place after all. So along with my drug use I started back into crime full time, not caring what happened. I knew I was either going back to prison or the graveyard, and whichever came first was all right with me.

But now, back in prison and treatment, I'm realizing that things don't have to be that way. I'm thankful for the treatment community here that's helping me deal with my life, sober.

◆

Michael N., St. Clair Correctional Facility, Alabama
Robbery
99 years

DECEMBER 5

I'M A 21-YEAR-OLD first offender, locked up and in recovery for the first time. I caught my case at the age of 19. I was an alcoholic, but at the time I couldn't admit to myself that I had a problem. I knew the things I was doing weren't right, but I thought I was just having fun. I had problems that I didn't know how to handle, so I used alcohol and reefer and violence to keep from dealing with them.

In recovery, whenever I have a problem I go to someone here and talk about it instead of turning to the negative escape routes I used to turn to. I now realize that suppressing my problems with drugs and alcohol won't make them go away, it only makes them worse.

If I turn my negative thoughts into positive ones and deal with the problems honestly, life begins to change for the better. I believe that is happening today, and it will keep happening as long as I am honest with myself and others.

◆

Winfred F., St. Clair Correctional Facility, Alabama
Attempted murder
'0 years

AFTER A LONG run from myself and my responsibility to my family came the time when I could think somewhat clearly again. Sitting in a cold and lonely cell, I got to find the truth within myself. I was at my all-time low. It was at this time that I got to find the Higher Power I was hearing about in A.A.

I am in prison for taking the life of someone I called a friend. That act took me down to the point when I started thinking about taking my own life. Thinking this I cried out, got down on my knees, and began to pray about my life. I felt that I had lost all hope. But I kept crying out and praying.

I found that the end was actually my beginning. I found hope in prayer. I begin to read the N.A. books, and my bad feeling started to pass even though the dreams of getting high kept coming.

It has been three years now from the day I began to emerge from my low point. Even the dreams of getting high have passed. When I found hope and something to live for — my family, my sons, and myself — I came to trust God, my Higher Power, would take the lead.

Never give up hope. Hope and trust *can* lead to healing. We must first get down to find a way up. I know, I am living proof.

◆

Julius W., St. Clair Correctional Facility, Alabama
Murder
Life

DECEMBER 7

FROM DAY ONE in the rehab program, everyone noticed I covered up all of my feelings with anger. It was the feeling I was most comfortable with, because it kept me from showing my true feelings. I was afraid to show how I really felt on the inside, and it caused me a lot of pain to deal with my issues.

For years I didn't have the courage to talk about my problems to others, and it seemed as if no one cared. After I started tearing down my wall of anger, I started letting out my true feelings that had been bottled up inside for a long time. I feel like I have had a great weight taken off of me.

I am just starting my recovery. I had to be willing to help myself before anyone else could help me.

◆

Van H., St. Clair Correctional Facility, Alabama
Burglary, Theft, Escape
15 years

I'M A REROUNDER as far as incarceration goes, but I'm in treatment for the first time. Since I've been in treatment I've taken an honest look at myself. Part of the therapy I've encountered is a long-term course on positive mental attitude. It was through this course that I came in contact with one of the greatest powers in the world, the power of choice.

So much of my life has revolved around doing things in order to be accepted or because I felt other people's choices were the right ones. But the best choice is the choice I make myself. Even if it is not the right choice, it will help me learn to make better ones.

I believe many of us do things we wouldn't have done had we taken time to evaluate the situation. We can either choose to do the same thing again because we know it may get noticed by someone, or we can choose to do something else because it is the best thing to do. Just remember, the choice is yours.

◆

Darrell M., St. Clair Correctional Facility, Alabama
Murder
Life without parole

DECEMBER 9

THIS IS MY sixth time in prison for alcohol-related crimes. I never really had a lasting desire to change my way of life, which was doing drugs, drinking, and running the streets. I had a family and a good job, so I simply lived two separate lifestyles. I didn't have any goals or a sense of direction. I didn't want to let go of either lifestyle. In other words, I never wanted to change.

When I had the car wreck and killed a man, I hit my bottom. I never thought this would happen to me.

While serving time at another maximum-security prison, I applied for treatment for two reasons: first, I figured it would look good on my record, and second, I really did want to go out into the real world and live clean.

That's all it takes to get started — a sincere desire to change your way of living.

Since being in treatment I've come a long way toward understanding myself, where and how my problems came about, and how to effectively deal with them now and when I return to society. In my groups, I'm getting in touch with feelings that I've buried for years. By doing that, I'm beginning to understand myself. Once things are understood, they can be dealt with much more effectively.

◆

Danny O., St. Clair Correctional Facility, Alabama
Vehicular homicide
15 years

I'M 20 YEARS old and I have a 10-year sentence. When I was 15 years old my mother died and I was the one who found her dead. At the time, I was in a group home. I've blamed myself for five years for my mother's death. I figured if I wouldn't have been in a group home, I could have saved her life.

I became very angry and resentful. I rejected all of my family. My hate grew so much I tried to kill myself three times. I hated myself and everyone around me. I was always telling people that my family gave up on me. I finally realized they never for one minute gave up on me; I gave up on myself and everyone around me.

It's taken me five years and coming to prison to realize what my life was turning out to be. By being in this program and in recovery, I realize that how I choose to live my life is the greatest freedom I will ever have. By applying what I've been through, my life is 110 percent fuller. I feel good about myself and others around me. I feel I am loved and I can give love. I love my life and the fullness I have in it now.

◆

James F., St. Clair Correctional Facility, Alabama
Assault
10 years

DECEMBER 11

I HAVE BEEN in treatment a little over 60 days and things have been much different than I expected. Besides meeting some great people, I have gotten in touch with some feelings and dredged up some memories that I hid for years with alcohol and drugs. I also learned some things about myself that have hurt a great deal, which I hope will be beneficial to me in the rest of my recovery.

I cannot say that I am cured by any stretch of the imagination. I know that my recovery will be a lifelong struggle, but I'm slowly learning some of the reasons why I have destroyed my life the way I have. I have not enjoyed everything that I have gone through here, and I probably will go through a lot more ups and downs and pain dealing with my issues, but I have come to the realization that I don't have anything to lose but a lot of misery. By going through treatment and staying sober, I have a lot to gain, but it has to be my choice. And it will take a lot of effort on my part.

◆

Joseph R., St. Clair Correctional Facility, Alabama
Robbery
12 years

THERE ARE A lot of stumbling blocks in recovery, and we have to learn to cope with the harsh situations that come our way. Most of us fail because of stressful situations. We need to put that negative energy we apply to destroying our lives into more positive and productive actions. It takes a lot of energy to go on a seven-day binge, but that same time and energy can just as easily be applied to living sober and addiction-free.

It is essential that we recovering addicts learn to cope with our old ways of thinking. Another important thing is to avoid high-risk situations in general. We need to change old friends, old hangouts, old thought patterns, and tend to our recovery. Remember, the disease is progressive.

Become active in recovery. Choose a Higher Power. Keep in mind that we cannot do it alone.

◆

Charles B., St. Clair Correctional Facility, Alabama
Murder, burglary, Possession of narcotics
45 years

DECEMBER 13

MY PERSONAL EXPERIENCE is that I get more help by fighting the addiction, not the system. Some things the counselors and other recovery addicts say may sound crazy, but they know what they're talking about. They are recovering, and they are using the tools that helped them.

I apply everything that is taught to me. I am very serious, and I motivate myself to practice new tactics that I learn in treatment. For instance, whenever I feel a lust for drugs coming on, I get with a friend and talk about it — someone who understands clearly where I'm coming from.

You have to be serious about changing your life. If not, then all the treatment and drilling in the world won't help. I practice thinking about the negative side of drugs. Usually my euphoric thinking reminds me of all the good things that happened in my drug-using days. I reverse it by thinking what it actually cost me, who I've hurt in the process, and where it always leaves me.

◆

Alford F., St. Clair Correctional Facility, Alabama
Burglary, Probation violation
1 year

I WISH TO write about how important it is to vigorously apply the Twelve Steps to my life. I took them too lightly and relapsed several times.

I had heard many times in meetings that our disease is progressive, and it's true. During my last relapse I had an auto accident that killed my wife. So here I am in prison again, with a manslaughter charge. By taking the program and the seriousness of my disease too lightly, my wife lost her life. Her death finally opened my eyes to how serious addiction really is.

My advice is to treat addiction as a life-or-death situation, and believe it when someone tells you the disease gets worse. The Twelve Steps of A.A. and N.A. do work, you just have to apply them vigorously and stay on top of your program. Because once you think you are cured, it slips up on you and hits you much harder than before.

◆

Ricky H., St. Clair Correctional Facility, Alabama
Criminal negligent homicide
27 years

DECEMBER 15

DURING MY THREE trips to prison I always came up short in the patience department. I despised waiting for anything. When I wanted something, I wanted it right now.

After being in treatment and recovery for two years, I've found that patience is one of the keys to recovery. Now, the day before my release on parole, I can look back and see all that I've missed in life because I refused to show any patience.

I finally have found what I've been missing — myself. Just by slowing down and waiting on things to come to me, I have a solid foundation to work from when I'm released.

Take life one day at a time and you'll get exactly what you're looking for. Life itself.

◆

Ronnie R., St. Clair Correctional Facility, Alabama
Receiving stolen property
30 years

I WAS DRIVEN by crack cocaine, and it led me to commit all kinds of crimes. The only reason I'm here now is because through it all, God stayed with me. I should have been dead.

The spiritual aspect of my recovery plays a most important role. My spiritual awakening took place in jail when I realized the seriousness of my crimes and the time I was facing once again. I knew that I needed to change, and that God was the only one capable of giving me the help I needed.

It's been three years since I've used any kind of drugs. It hasn't been easy. I'm constantly struggling with my addiction, and I rely on my Higher Power every minute of every day to help me overcome the temptation of doing drugs. In working my recovery program, it is mandatory that I look to God. My old ways of doing things just didn't work, and I can't afford to get out and fall back into the same lifestyle again.

◆

LaBarron D., St. Clair Correctional Facility, Alabama
Robbery
3 years

DECEMBER 17

TREATMENT IS LIKE an awakening of one's self. It makes you aware of problems you didn't really know you had, and it also gives you some answers on how to deal with them.

I have been in treatment about three years now. At first, I had many problems to deal with. One of them was stress. Because of treatment I have come up with a number ways to deal with stress.

Here are some of the things I do: I do something each day that gives me energy, something only for me that I love to do. I've become more aware of the demands I place on myself, my environment, and others to be different than they are, so I'm learning to reduce my demands. I create and maintain my personal support system. Professionals help when I feel unable to cope. I also take time to be alone on a regular basis to listen to my heart, to reevaluate my goals, and to prioritize my activities. It's been suggested that I do one thing at a time, keeping my mind focused on the present. Doing things more slowly, more intentionally, and with more awareness and respect also helps with stress.

Recovery gives insight to my problems and gives me an answer to them. I want recovery to always be a part of my life. I've experienced so many negative things, it's wonderful to be on the positive side.

Warren E., Graham Correctional Center, Illinois
Robbery
11 years

THE EASIEST EMOTION for me to feel is anger. Up until nine months ago when I came into recovery, my anger had done nothing but escalate. I was a walking time bomb. I felt that my anger was justified, because there are so many things that can happen in a day's time in prison to make me extremely angry.

I have discovered that there are just as many positive things that happen. The only change is, I look for the positive now. I never looked for anything but the negative in the past.

Don't get me wrong, I still get angry, but I see things from a whole new perspective now. I feel 100 percent better about my new attitude, and so do my friends and family.

◆

Doug A., St. Clair Correctional Facility, Alabama
Murder
Life without parole

DECEMBER 19

RECOVERY IS A hard road to follow. The first thing I had to do was realize I had hit bottom. Even in prison, sometimes we don't see the bottom coming until we realize where we are. It took me seven years.

After finally hitting bottom, I could see the top. Getting there is a long-term goal that I will have to strive for the rest of my life. I am an alcoholic and drug addict, and the only way to stay sober is to tell my story to others who have the same problem and believe in myself.

I believe Step One of the Twelve Steps, admitting I am powerless over alcohol, is the most important. It gives me a future to look to. And A.A. gives me friends who love me to help me get there.

◆

James C., St. Clair Correctional Facility, Alabama
Manslaughter
Life

GROWING UP, I always felt rejected by those I wanted to be closest to. Because of this I could never accept myself. Therefore, I could never love myself.

Later, if my peers couldn't accept and love me, then I figured I was unacceptable and unworthy of love. I began trying to act like others. But when this failed, my self-worth dropped even lower. I began to hate myself. I tried emulating my idols for years, but I finally reached the point when I couldn't do it anymore. I had to be myself.

The problem was, I didn't know who I was. After several years of suffering from the pain and frustration of not being able to find myself, I accepted that I could not do it alone. I entered the treatment program, which was the turning point in my life. Through the group process I am beginning to discover myself. And the caring people in my group are giving me the encouragement I need to accept myself, and the love I need to love myself.

◆

Richard K., St. Clair Correctional Facility, Alabama
Murder
Life without parole

DECEMBER 21

I HAD NEVER thought of sex as an addiction. But little by little, like any addiction, it progressed until it had consumed my entire being. I found myself helpless against something much bigger than I was. I needed help; I couldn't stand alone against this obsession.

In recovery I've discovered that the only way out is within. Once I understood the addictive process, I learned I wasn't powerless over its grasp. This was only the beginning of a struggle that forced me to learn about myself. The recovery program gave me the tools, the groups gave me the guidance, and my Higher Power gave me the strength. And, as the addiction had once grown little by little, so did my recovery. Bit by bit, day by day, step by step, I began to gain and maintain new hope for my life.

The journey of a thousand miles began with one step. How grateful I am that I took that first step.

◆

James T., St. Clair Correctional Facility, Alabama
Rape
Life

I WAS A slow learner in grade school so I quit at an early age and started running with a bad crowd. I felt confident only when I was doing crazy things; it was hard to mess up a disaster.

After talking about my past in treatment, I saw that a lot of the negative messages I got as a child had stuck with me. Self-doubt was one of my major issues in recovery.

I've just recently earned my G.E.D. and am in my third quarter of college. As I look back, I can see how my lack of education played a major role in my self-doubt and lack of confidence.

I look at how I felt about myself then and how I feel now. Today, my life consists of doing everything I can to better myself. I'm taking risks and making mistakes, but I'm learning from them in the process.

◆

Larry G., St. Clair Correctional Facility, Alabama
Robbery
Life without parole

DECEMBER 23

THE ONE CONCEPT that has helped me the most in treatment is, "You get what your hand calls for." This concept taught me that if I'm not honest with myself and others, treatment won't work. If I'm honest, I will recover.

Thank you for taking the time to read this. I hope it will be of some help to you.

◆

Charles G., St. Clair Correctional Facility, Alabama
Kidnapping
Life

I'M 38 YEARS old and have served over 21 years in the Alabama prison system. I've been through some rough times in some terrible places. Being in recovery makes all my past experiences look easy.

I entered treatment with the wrong intentions. I just wanted to get out of prison. I don't regret or deny that, but I do want to say that the course has changed. I've discovered problems that I wasn't aware existed and I've met a guy I never knew — myself. Drugs and prison life had numbed my feelings and covered up my emotions for so long I forgot how it felt to care and be cared for. I'm not going to waste time regretting the past because it now serves as a learning experience to direct me in the future.

In here we say it's okay to make a mistake as long as we learn from it. My life has been full of mistakes and bad choices, but I never learned anything from them. That also is changing. I can see a better me. Not only do I have a new direction and goals to strive toward, I also have confidence in myself. Getting off drugs allowed me to see myself just as I am. Treatment allows me to understand myself so I can love and respect the person I'll live with forever.

◆

Phillip W., St. Clair Correctional Facility, Alabama
Murder
30 years

DECEMBER 25

THE LAST TIME I was arrested, I knew that I had to do something to get out of prison and stay out once and for all. So coming in this time I didn't do any of the things that I had done previously. I didn't do any drugs or gamble or any of the other negative things you can get into in prison, but it didn't seem to be enough.

This treatment program filled in what was missing. I have found that the problem wasn't just the drugs and alcohol. After getting in touch with my past and dealing with it openly and honestly, I found that I feel better about myself and what it is I need to do to stay out of prison.

Getting in touch with my feelings and expressing them openly has given me a confidence that I never thought possible. The relationships that I have with my family and kids are not ideal, but they are better. I am more responsible now, my self-esteem is up, and I am growing as a person.

This program works. I hope to get out and help rebuild the community that I once tried to destroy. I have a lot of guilt and shame to deal with, but with the help of this program I will overcome my past. I have turned my life around. Things that I have no control over, I have turned over to my Higher Power.

David H., St. Clair Correctional Facility, Alabama
Robbery
Life

DECEMBER 26

BEFORE COMING INTO a treatment program, I knew nothing about addiction, compulsive behavior, dysfunctional homes, addictive personalities, childhood messages, or any other links to addiction. I had many questions I was desperately seeking answers to, and in 19 months I've finally started getting them answered and am coming to understand what recovery means to me.

I am multiply addicted, and therapy and treatment are helping me to get clean and stay clean. Therapy is a lifelong process for the successful recovering addict. And thanks to intense programs like this one, I've learned some tools for maintaining personal recovery. These tools include responsibility, patience, spirituality, self-disclosure, and relationship building. The first stage of recovery for me was obtaining these tools. The hard part is learning to use them for the rest of my life.

◆

James H., St. Clair Correctional Facility, Alabama
Rape
Life

DECEMBER 27

THROUGH THE RECOVERY process, I discovered I had a fear of people, places, and things. In order to deal with this fear, I used to use drugs and alcohol to give me courage. But that courage was only a myth.

Intensive therapy gives me the knowledge and the tools to use when things arrive in my life that I'm fearful of. At this point in my life, I live one day at a time. Yes, I still have fear of certain things, but it's okay. I know I don't have to use to be able to deal with any of them.

I give thanks to my Higher Power for giving me the courage, wisdom, and understanding to accept treatment and to get on with my life.

◆

Robert H., St. Clair Correctional Facility, Alabama
Murder
Life without parole

THIS IS MY fourth time in prison and it seems this is the trip that will keep me here. Getting sentenced to life without parole made me realize that something had to be wrong with my behavior and thinking.

Drugs had a lot to do with it, but it goes deeper than that. It has a lot to do with my attitude toward myself and others. There was not much respect for either. I didn't know how to love, and I was an angry person. But I can learn to love others and myself through treatment.

Just being honest and truly admitting what hurts me and trying to learn new ways of doing things is what it's all about for me. There are still times when I am angry about being in this situation, but I'm learning how to deal with my anger instead of lashing out against others.

◆

Buddy L., St. Clair Correctional Facility, Alabama
Murder, Burglary, Possession of cocaine
Life without parole

DECEMBER 29

I HAVE BEEN in recovery for 16 months. I am now in a position to work with others as they come into the orientation phase of the program. I have to remind myself daily not to bombard these people with too much information too fast. The fun part of recovery is discovering your true identity with the loving guidance of others rather than with someone telling you what your problems are. I allow newcomers, and myself, to make mistakes and learn from them.

One of the most common things I see is new people coming into recovery and starting to feel their feelings again. They feel sorry for what they have done. Most of the time people have had such a bad track record of making false promises that apologizing isn't enough. They have to prove through actions and attitude that they are changing.

I have seen many relationships reborn through the recovery process. If we do what's right for the right reasons, good things will come back to us. We are not victims of circumstances, we are creators of circumstances.

◆

David V., St. Clair Correctional Facility, Alabama
Burglary, Forgery, Escape
23 years

A few years ago when I was 19, I was walking on Alabama's death row. I remember feeling desperately lonely, and I knew that if I did not make some changes in my life that I would be sitting in a one-man cell caged up like a wild animal with nothing to look forward to but death itself.

I started drinking at the age of nine and did not stop until the day I was arrested and charged with capital murder. Even then I didn't really stop, I only slowed down. I put little value on human life. I was so driven by my addictions, I was not capable of caring, not even for the most important people in my life.

My recovery has been a slow and very painful process. The hardest thing for me was to admit that I truly was powerless over my addictions which ranged from pills and reefer to alcohol to sex. Before I came into recovery, I didn't know what it was like to live without those things in my life. I had to take all of those bad things out and replace them with good things. Recovery is the way. Even if the road is not a smooth one, just think of where we would be without it.

◆

Jimmy S., St. Clair Correctional Facility, Alabama
Murder
30 years

DECEMBER 31

I HAVE A lot of fear about returning to society and to the old game and my old crowd. The world outside of these prison walls never changes. It always remains the same.

The change has to come from within me. Like the Serenity Prayer says, I need to ask for serenity to accept the things I cannot change and the courage to change the things I can. I can't change society, but I can change myself.

◆

David H., Graham Correctional Center, Illinois
Aggravated battery
4 years

About Hazelden Publishing

As part of the Hazelden Betty Ford Foundation, Hazelden Publishing offers both cutting-edge educational resources and inspirational books. Our print and digital works help guide individuals in treatment and recovery, and their loved ones. Professionals who work to prevent and treat addiction also turn to Hazelden Publishing for evidence-based curricula, digital content solutions, and videos for use in schools, treatment programs, correctional programs, and electronic health records systems. We also offer training for implementation of our curricula.

Through published and digital works, Hazelden Publishing extends the reach of healing and hope to individuals, families, and communities affected by addiction and related issues.

For more information about Hazelden publications,
please call 800-328-9000 or visit us online at
hazelden.org/bookstore.

Hazelden Publishing offers an array of daily meditation books, in print and e-book formats, to be read in the morning, at night, or anytime. Whether one is a recovering addict, sponsor, or counselor, there is a meditation book suitable for all. Our books cover recovery topics pertinent to everyone (*Twenty-Four Hours a Day, Keep It Simple, The Promise of a New Day*), as well as daily meditations written especially for men (*Touchstones*), women (*Each Day a New Beginning*), teens (*Twenty-Four Hours for Teens*), adult children (*Days of Healing, Days of Joy*), families (*Today's Gift*), those dealing with codependency (*The Language of Letting Go*), mental health issues (*A Restful Mind*), eating disorders (*Inner Harvest*), sex addiction (*Answers in the Heart*), and more.

Hazelden Publishing meditation books are available at fine bookstores everywhere. To order from Hazelden Publishing, call **800-328-9000** or visit **hazelden.org/bookstore**.